The Destruction of the U-Boat Menace

"They are too near to be great,
but our children shall understand.
When and how our fate
Was changed, and by whose hand."

"Our children shall measure their worth,
We are content to be blind . . .
But we know that we walk on a new-born earth,
With the saviours of mankind."

(From Kipling's "Battle of Jutland.")

The Destruction of the U-Boat Menace

Admiral Sims and the Anti-Submarine War, 1917-18

ILLUSTRATED

Simsadus: London

John Langdon Leighton

With a Short Biography of Admiral Sims

by Cora W. Rowell

LEONAUR

The Destruction of the U-Boat Menace
Admiral Sims and the Anti-Submarine War, 1917-18
Simsadus: London
by John Langdon Leighton
With a Short Biography of Admiral Sims
by Cora W. Rowell

ILLUSTRATED

FIRST EDITION

Leonaur is an imprint of Oakpast Ltd
Copyright in this form © 2022 Oakpast Ltd

ISBN: 978-1-915234-80-3 (hardcover)
ISBN: 978-1-915234-81-0 (softcover)

http://www.leonaur.com

Contents

To My Mother
As a Mark, not a Measure,
Of the Love of a Devoted Son.

Foreword

How unfit and how unworthy a choice have I made of myself to undertake a work of this mixture, mine own reason though exceeding weak, hath sufficiently resolved me.

Thus, wrote Sir Walter Raleigh in the preface to his *History of the World*. By profession I am not an author nor a naval officer, and yet I have undertaken to write a brief narrative of the American Navy in Europe during the Great War. Would that the talents of Sir Walter were at my command—but I shall mention him no further lest by drawing him into the matter I flatter myself. I can but thank him for the apt way in which he has expressed my sentiments. In these days of limitless rumours, twice-told tales of glory, startling revelations, hitherto undisclosed facts, and much misinformation, I hope this work will find a place. It is not official, and as sanction has not been sought, it is published without it.

One morning in March, 1918, I found myself a member of the Intelligence Section of Admiral Sims' Staff in London. The work in which I then joined and continued during the remainder of the war, and for several months thereafter, was so totally absorbing in its interests that, upon my return to this country, I put what I had witnessed into writing. Were my powers of expression not so limited, I know the reader would be as easily absorbed in learning why and how great things were done as I was in watching their development from day to day. If you are in quest of the Romance of the War, I recommend to you the voluminous literature that has been written thereon. In my own experience, the romance of the war *began* on April 16, 1917, the day on which I left Harvard University, and donned the uniform of a seaman; it *ceased* the following morning when I was aroused from pleasant slumbers at 5 a. m. to wash the deck.

Those of us who joined the ranks of the navy in this war found ourselves playing a new role in the comedy or drama of life. We left a universe of freedom and entered a world in which hours for smoking, shore leave, uniforms to be worn, and the adjustment of our lives were prescribed by autocratic law and regulations. We chafed under our restrictions and blamed those who enforced them in their tyrannical attitude. We did not realise that in an officer's orders, or the manner in which we were addressed, there was nothing of the personal; these men were but enforcing that splendid institution, the code of discipline.

But as I now look back and see before me the characters of those officers with whom I came in contact, I doubt whether any finer or more manly group of men exists. They were educated and trained to know the true meaning of duty, responsibility, and devotion; they were brisk in their manner, quick to act, severe in their judgments, and, at heart, human.

A word in explanation of my title is pertinent. Simsadus: London was the cable address of the American Navy in Europe, or. In other words, Admiral Sims' Headquarters in London. The word "Simsadus" dissected, means—"Sims—Admiral—U. S."

John Langdon Leighton.

Monadnock Farms,
Monadnock, New Hampshire.
September, 1919

CHAPTER 1

The General Submarine Situation in April, 1917

Perhaps some of us will recall that in the first week in May, 1917, we were informed by an official statement of the British Admiralty, that during the previous month of April 875,000 tons of Allied and neutral shipping had been sent to the bottom of the sea by German submarines. This information was not given to the British people, for it would have been a more staggering blow to them than any other "war truth" yet disclosed. It might have stunned us likewise, had we not at that time been the possessors of optimistic hopes and rallying hearts in an adventure which seemed necessarily successful by our mere participation in it. To a certain extent our point of view turned out to be correct, but at that time it was far from justified.

The submarine situation in April, 1917, was briefly this. Germany had constructed 213 submarines; she had lost 55, leaving her a total of 158 underwater craft, with which in April she sank 875,000 tons of shipping. She was building an average of six or seven per month, while her losses averaged but three or four. The total tonnage of the world before the war was about 32,000,000 tons, of which by the end of April over 7,500,000 tons had already been sunk. Losses at the rate of 1,000,000 tons per month, which Germany had promised she would sink, and which she virtually did in April, meant that in the course of a few months, the Allies would be in a state of starvation. It was a simple problem of arithmetic to calculate the conclusion of the war in Germany's favour.

England, the greatest shipbuilding nation of the world, was not meeting the losses by new construction. Her shipyards were burdened with repair work on vessels injured by submarine attacks, and very much overcrowded in the construction of new naval craft; and the continuous demand for men in the army caused a chronic shortage of labour. It was a bad position in which Great Britain, against whom the brunt of the submarine campaign was directed, found herself, and a disheartening one when one considers that the construction of a ship takes many months and its destruction by a submarine but a few moments.

The United States was launching a tremendous shipbuilding programme which looked promising on paper, but many realised that a non-shipbuilding nation, however great in wealth, man-power, and resources, could not be converted into a great shipbuilding nation in less than two or three years. And the critical period of the war was to come in four or five months! in view of all this, the leaders of Great Britain in May, 1917, looked upon the failure of the Allies through the success of German submarines as a possible reality. What then was to save the cause of the Allies? The checking of the submarine successes, one may answer; but how was this to be done, and how was the submarine menace being met at that time?

At a rough estimate the Royal Navy was handling about 80% of the war against the submarine in all areas of submarine operations, such as the North Sea, the English Channel, all waters west of England and Ireland, and the West Coast of France; also in the Mediterranean, where the submarine campaign was pressed with the same virulence as marked its operations in Atlantic waters. England had at this time about 200 destroyers in commission, of which 100 were on duty with the Grand Fleet in the North Sea.

As long as the German Fleet kept up its threat of fight, the British Grand Fleet had to remain intact. Another fifty destroyers were in service in the English Channel, across which every British Tommy, his "Bully Beef," and his ammunition had to pass to get to France. A few more were employed in the Mediterranean. This left but a meagre two dozen to patrol all waters West of the United Kingdom, the Irish Sea, and to the South and North of Ireland, etc. The duties of all British destroyers were greater than they could really shoulder, and many of them, after three years of war, were in urgent need of extensive repairs.

These two dozen which were stationed at Milford Haven, Plymouth, and Holyhead were responsible for the efficacious patrol of all the waters west of the British isles. Their patrol system was briefly this. The waters were theoretically marked off into large squares or areas, and to each area a destroyer was assigned; with so few destroyers the squares were of course very large; and yet they were supposed to patrol their square incessantly to keep the submarines down, and, if possible, to attack them. This put the destroyer in a position of little value, for as the submarine could see the destroyer long before the destroyer could see the submarine, and as submarines were looking for merchant ships, not for destroyers, the submarine could very easily avoid the anti-submarine vessels.

The system worked out disastrously and therefore was discarded and a new plan adopted. All incoming ships were now directed to come into the Western British Ports, along any one of four or five different and designated lanes, which the destroyers were to keep as free from submarines as possible. An incoming or outgoing ship, while passing along one of these lanes, would be picked up by a destroyer and escorted for some distance, and then left alone until she was picked up again. This system was an attempt at a Convoy system, but was successful only in that while one escorted ship arrived safely at its port, probably another two or three were unescorted, and therefore open to attack.

It worked out better than its predecessor, but there still was very much to be desired. The Naval Authorities knew that a Convoy system would be better, for it had been used in the English Channel since 1914, and not a British Tommy had lost his life in crossing.

★★★★★★★★★★

The Convoy system was a procedure in which several merchant ships would be assembled together, and then proceed under the protection of destroyers towards their destination. The principle of the Convoy dates back to the age of Merchant Caravans in the Far East.

★★★★★★★★★★

The Convoy system was a logical remedy to the submarine menace, if—there were a sufficient number of destroyers to serve as escorts.

It is true that the Admiralty had pressed and was pressing into service every available self-propelled vessel. These vessels, which were trawlers, fishing boats, and ferry boats, did noble work, and as Kipling has put it:

In Lowestoft a boat was laid,
Mark well what I do say!
And she was built for the herring trade.
But she has gone a-rovin', a-rovin', a-rovin',
The Lord knows where!

They gave her government coal to burn.
And a Q. F. gun at bow and stern.

13

And sent her out a-rovin', a-rovin', a-rovin',
The Lord knows where!

Her skipper was mate of a bucko ship
Which always killed one man per trip.
So, he is used to rovin', a-rovin', a-rovin',
The Lord knows where!

Her mate was skipper of a chapel in Wales,
And so he fights in topper and tails—
Religi-ous tho' rovin', a-rovin', a-rovin',
The Lord knows where!

Her engineer is fifty-eight.
So, he's prepared to meet his fate.
Which ain't unlikely rovin', a-rovin', a-rovin',
The Lord knows where!

Her leading-stoker's seventeen,
So, he don't know what the Judgments mean,
Unless he cops 'em rovin', a-rovin', a-rovin',
The Lord knows where!

Her cook was chef in the Lost Dogs' Home,
Mark well what I do say!
And I'm sorry for Fritz when they all come
A-rovin', a-rovin', a-roarin' and a-rovin',
Round the North Sea rovin',
The Lord knows where!

But as the submarine war continued and the fair weather and long summer nights were approaching, the submarines moved further out into deep waters where trawlers and paddle steamers could not venture. Just how seriously the demand for anti-submarine vessels was, at this time, has never been appreciated, for the arrival of the American destroyers in European waters added the desired number and changed the whole aspect of the situation. With the coming of these vessels in April, and more in May and June, new hopes came to those who knew that the sword of Damocles, disguised as a submarine, had been hanging over the heads of France, Italy, Great Britain, and America.

CHAPTER 2

Admiral Sims in London

During the latter part of March, 1917, Rear Admiral Sims was ordered from the U. S. Naval War College in Newport, R. I., of which he was President, to Washington. After conferences and instructions from Secretary Daniels, he and his *aide*, Commander J.V. B. Babcock, prior to America's Declaration of War, proceeded to London in civilian clothes aboard the steamship *New York*. They arrived in Liverpool on April 10th, and were met by a special train and Rear Admiral Hope, R. N., the Envoy of the British Admiralty. Admiral Sims had been sent to Europe to confer with the British Naval Authorities as to the best manner in which the American Navy might throw its weight into the anti-submarine struggle and to command such American vessels as might be sent to Europe.

As an American naval officer of high rank, he was well received in London, but there were also other reasons for the extremely warm reception extended to him. Admiral Sims was no mere acquaintance to the Royal Navy, for he had served in many stations in Europe, and as *attaché* in some of the great capitals, during which appointments he had made many friends in the Royal Navy. The higher officers of the Royal Navy looked upon him as America's greatest naval officer, and they all were familiar with the story of his statement to a gathering of British naval officers in 1910, in which he said that if the Royal Navy ever needed the support of the American Navy, that support would be extended.

For this remark he had been censured by President Taft; but the censure had been forgotten, and the remark had lived. Here was the same American officer, who years before had expressed an appreciation of Great Britain, and made a prophecy that the U. S. Navy would support the Royal Navy in time of trouble. The prophecy had come true and its author was to be the leader of the American forces, at the time when the fate of England and the world were in the balance.

A few words here about Admiral Sims are pertinent. His career as a naval officer had been brilliant and he became a marked man on three different occasions. In 1905 he had set his heart so firmly upon the necessity of an improvement in the gunnery of the American Navy that, when his plans were refused by the Navy Department, he took the matter up with President Roosevelt himself, who immediately saw the value of Lieutenant-Commander Sims' schemes, and had the whole gunnery system of the U. S. Navy altered.

He became a marked man again in 1909, when, with the rank of Commander, he was ordered to serve as the commanding officer of the U. S. S. "*Minnesota.*" This was the first time in the history of the American Navy that an officer below the rank of captain had commanded a first class attleship. And then in 1910 he made his famous speech to the British naval officers. For these reasons, Admiral Sims was the American naval officer most widely known to the Royal Navy. He was the most welcome.

His mission was to discuss with the British Naval Authorities the plans by which the efforts of the American Navy would be of the greatest value against the submarines or U-boats. Upon his arrival in London, he had long and pertinent conferences with the leaders of the Government, with the Prime Minister and other Cabinet Ministers, and the Lords of the Admiralty. In these conferences he requested that no information be withheld from him, regardless of how secret or pessimistic that information might be. The results were interesting. Having made himself thoroughly familiar with existing conditions, he wrote home to the Secretary of the Navy, emphasising two points.

First, he pointed out that the Allies were in a fair way to succumb to Germany's sea policy unless the United States could furnish merchant "bottoms" in the near future, and Military and Naval aid immediately. The second point of interest was the policy which he then and there laid down, and from which he never deviated, for the American Navy in Europe; namely, that in order to be of the greatest use, the American warships which were to come to European waters, should operate as a part of the British Forces, and their employment and disposition supplement the weaker spots of the British Naval Organisation.

In this way he sacrificed fame for himself; for how splendid it would have been to be the gallant "Sea Admiral" of the American Navy, such as Beatty was in the Royal Navy. Instead, he saw that to

16

have the U. S. Navy in Europe as a distinct and separate organisation would only lead to delays and complications; he saw that the policy already mentioned, in which the two navies could become merged into one, would be better. Thus, he took his place as the first great Allied chief to appreciate the value of unity of command.

He immediately established himself in London that his headquarters might eventually function as an integral part of the British Admiralty. The scope of the Naval War was wide, demanding that efforts be concentrated and not scattered. Naturally, London offered facilities of easy contact with all theatres of operation, particularly as regards communication. He realised that his communication system would be a vital factor in the efficient management of the U. S. Naval Forces, because of the great distance which would separate him from his bases and from Washington. In May he requested the services of a young lieutenant-commander of the regular navy named Blakeslee, who came over from Washington in August, and this officer with a vision of the potential activities of the Forces to come under the admiral's command, established probably the finest communication system of any Allied belligerent organisation in the war.

★★★★★★★★★★

The news of Lt. Commander Blakeslee's death in March, 1919 in Paris was keenly felt by all who knew him, and realised what a great service he had rendered. In December, 1918, he was ordered to Paris and there established the Communication system used by the American delegates at the Peace Conference.

★★★★★★★★★★

By means of this system, members of Admiral Sims' staff could communicate in code with any of the bases, later established, whether at Murmansk, in Russia, or at the island of Corfu in the Mediterranean, with only a few hours intervening between cables sent and answers received.

However, before Admiral Sims became worried over the efficient management of his forces, he devoted all his energy and experience and resources towards the development of their future operations, *i.e.*, what were they to do? where were they to do it? and how should they do it? in adopting the policy that the United States Navy should supplement the weaker spots of the Royal Navy, he had made one reservation, that American vessels should primarily be engaged in anti-submarine warfare and that any portions of the Royal Navy not employed in fighting submarines, even though employed in the naval situation as a whole, would have to wait to be strengthened by American vessels, until the critical stage had passed. He took this stand because he believed that the anti-submarine forces needed help more critically than other units.

He believed that the American people would prefer to have their forces in Europe primarily fighting submarines because the submarine war had been the cause of America's entry into the struggle. This stand was readily understood, appreciated, and accepted by the Admiralty. In order properly to understand the future developments and ultimate activities of our forces, a closer view of the existing conditions and suggested remedies is interesting.

The tactics in fighting the submarine at the time of America's entry into the war have already been discussed, and I have shown that the presence of destroyers on patrol duty, here and there, was really of little value. They could hardly expect to find submarines resting quietly on the surface, and certainly could not locate them when submerged. If a destroyer happened to pick up a ship and escort her some distance, some good was being done, but while one was being escorted safely, probably another two were being sunk a few miles away. Thus, the time and effort spent in escorting one ship were all out of proportion to the value of one ship, as long as others were being destroyed in great numbers.

What was wanted was a system in which time, effort, and energy could be used to the best advantage; in other words, concentration of the material and resources at hand. Many suggestions for the improvement of conditions were made, and the suggestions were all of value. In the discussion which follows, however, it must be borne in mind that, with the lack of sufficient numbers of anti-submarine vessels, and destroyers in particular, the sinkings could not feasibly be lessened.

The first of the many methods suggested was the arming of merchant ships. This was looked upon far more favourably in this country than in England, where experience had shown that the presence of a gun on a merchant ship in no way protected it from being sunk. What it did do was to force the submarine to use a torpedo in sinking a ship. This meant that a submarine could destroy no greater number of ships than the number of torpedoes it could carry, and of course, such a doctrine carried with it a certain amount of virtue, but as a means of protecting ships from being sunk it was not successful.

Another method suggested was the use of mines and nets. This was not a new idea; it involved rather the development of a principle

18

already in use, for mines and nets have been used in all recent wars to hamper the movements of enemy ships. (In 1777 a chain was laid across the Hudson River south of West Point, to prevent the British vessels from going up the river.) As submarines operated on the high seas, and miles of open water could not be promiscuously sown with floating mines, their use had been restricted to such areas as the Dover Straits, the Eastern end of the North Sea, along the entrances to harbours, and such like. These fields proved effective to a certain extent, but many obstacles presented themselves. In the first place, wind and storm, ebb and flow, eventually would disrupt the mine field so much that it would often become just as much of a danger to Allied ships as to the enemy.

Also, a majority of U-boats were equipped with a mine and net-cutting device, which consisted of a sharp saw tooth instrument along the bows, aft of which, and along the whole length of the vessel, a strong steel wire above the periscope was stretched. A submarine running into a net would, by means of the saw tooth, cut one strand of the net open, and by means of the steel wire overhead, force its way through the gap. A submarine commander knowing of nets or a mine field, could bring his vessel to the surface or submerge to a great depth, and pass over or under safely. According to theory, the use of mines or nets would seem such an easy and successful method of checking submarine operations, but according to results, this was far from the case.

The U. S. Navy Department had since the beginning of the war, fostered a great plan for closing up the North Sea, and upon America's entry, the department suggested the scheme to the Admiralty through Admiral Sims. This mine field was to reach from Scotland to Norway, and was to prevent the egress of submarines into the high seas by way of the North of Scotland. The plan was good, very good and possible, and was eventually adopted, but in May, 1917, there were several excellent reasons for objecting to its construction at that time. When a mine field is laid, the mine-laying ships have to be protected from enemy assault, and after the field is laid, a constant watch has to be kept to prevent the enemy from raiding it and tearing it to bits with drags and towed nets.

Now a mine barrage, laid across the North Sea would have called for a long and constant patrol, which, unless the ships were capital ships—I mean battleships, cruisers, or battle cruisers—would have been no match for a heavy squadron of enemy vessels. He could have concentrated an attack on any one spot along a comparatively long and weak line of resistance, and have done the damage before the patrol vessels, whose assistance against a heavy squadron would have been of little use anyway, could appear upon the scene. A mine field, when once destroyed, if only in a small spot, is of no value until repaired. On the other hand, if the British were to employ capital ships as a protection to the mine field, these ships would have been open to torpedo attack.

It will be seen, then, that the laying of a mine field across the North Sea at that time, would have only made further demands upon the British naval vessels, of which there was already an acute shortage. But the chief objection raised, and Admiral Sims was right when he raised it, was based on the fact that the Allies did not have the mines with which to do it, and their construction would have taken months, at a time when the critical period of the submarine war was at hand! To have pinned great faith on this scheme at that time would have been folly.

The riddance of the submarine menace by mine fields was temporarily discarded, for after all is said and done, and in this peculiar and critical situation, mine fields were remedies of only a palliative sort and of secondary importance. Admiral Sims and the Admiralty authorities agreed on this point absolutely, and took their stand firmly that the submarine to be defeated had to be fought immediately where its strength lay.

The most promising suggestion offered was that of the Convoy System. It was by no means a new suggestion, for as said, the Royal Navy had used it during the two preceding years in escorting troop and supply ships to and from France. The Admiralty had considered putting a similar system into operation in the waters West of England, but realised that this could not be done with the lack of destroyers. The convoy would only be an improvement, *if*—there were a sufficient number of destroyers available for escort duty. If there were not, it would be far worse, for the available destroyers could handle but a small percentage of the total merchant traffic, thereby laying a very large proportion open to attack.

If the submarines had gained the information that the few available destroyers were escorting convoys, and no longer on patrol, a very free and open policy of still greater danger to the Allied ships would have followed. The mere fact that an occasional destroyer was out on patrol, tended to make the submarine exert a little caution at least;

if these occasional patrols had been withdrawn, nothing would have remained to hamper their ravages. With the arrival of the American destroyers in April, and more to come in May and June, a portion of the desired number of destroyers were added to the anti-submarine forces, and more detailed plans were drawn up for the formation of a Convoy System.

In drawing up these plans the officers of the Merchant Marine Service had to be consulted, and many of these old-time sea-going men were summoned to London to confer with the Admiralty authorities. Practically all of them declared themselves opposed to such a scheme. It must not be thought that in so doing their intentions were anything but of the best, for the desire for preservation of his ship is second nature to the merchant marine officer; and all of them heartily wished to contribute to the cause by the prevention of tonnage losses. Their objections were based on sincere argument, but in these they underestimated their own genius. They were all of the opinion that in convoys, where great ships would be huddled together in close formation, the losses through accidents would be too great.

They deplored their own abilities, and that of their ships, to keep in formation and not be a nuisance to each other. None of them had ever had the training of station keeping, as had the naval officer, and so they believed that efficient station keeping would be beyond their powers; they would far rather have run the risks of submarines themselves, protecting their ships by various antics or zigzags, and other manoeuvres of their own invention. Admiral Sims and a few British officers stepped into the breach of opinion thus formed, and declared that the merchant captain had underrated his abilities, and said that from what they had seen of the Merchant Marine, the average captain was very nearly as efficient in handling his ship as the average naval officer.

In this way a compromise was reached, and it was agreed to give the Convoy System a try out. This was done, and British destroyers at a later date proceeded out to sea some 150 miles, where they met some incoming ships from Gibraltar and escorted these back to Milford Haven. At the conclusion of this experiment the naval officers, whose destroyers had escorted the merchant ships, claimed that the station-keeping qualities of the merchantmen was good, and with a little more practice, might be rendered excellent. That settled the question, and definite plans for the establishment of the Convoy System were begun.

The values of the scheme were many. In the first place, the submarines had been attacking and sinking merchant ships without incurring any danger to themselves. If the ship thus attacked was not armed, the submarine could attack it by gun fire, or stop it, and then by sending members of its crew aboard the captive vessel, scuttle it or blow a hole in its bottom. In convoys, where large numbers of ships could be herded together and protected by a few destroyers, this procedure would not be possible; the submarine would have a fight for every ship sunk.

Furthermore, up to this time, submarines had roamed the open seas attacking merchant vessels, and avoiding destroyers and other anti-submarine craft; but in the Convoy System, in which the merchant ships and destroyers would proceed together, the submarines could not attack the ships without encountering protectors. The best locality in which to shoot a fox is near a hen yard; just so, the merchant ship was the submarine's prey, and in order to get the opportunity of attacking submarines, a few destroyers merely had to hang around, and the submarine would reveal itself sooner or later. This form of combating the submarine was really an offensive campaign against it, and that is what we wanted.

One of the cardinal principles of military strategy has always been that of concentration against the enemy. The Convoy System would supply this concentration perfectly. Before its adoption the anti-submarine effort had been scattered; a destroyer here and a destroyer there, and ships open to attack all over the place. The enemy, that is, the German submarines, had the concentration on his side in this state of affairs, while the Allied anti-submarine efforts were at sixes and sevens.

The Convoy System turned the tables; for with its adoption large numbers of ships protected by destroyers on all sides, would proceed together. In other words, the efforts of the destroyers were concentrated in their defence of shipping, while the efforts of the submarines, with fewer ships alone on the high seas, would have to be more varied and scattered. The introduction of this scheme then, was nothing more than a recognition and application of an old-time military principle.

There was one more point of great strength in this new system. It has already been pointed out how much Admiral Sims appreciated the necessity at this time of doing something, and of doing it quickly if the U-boat campaign was to be defeated; and how for that reason mining or net operations had been shelved, to be considered at a later

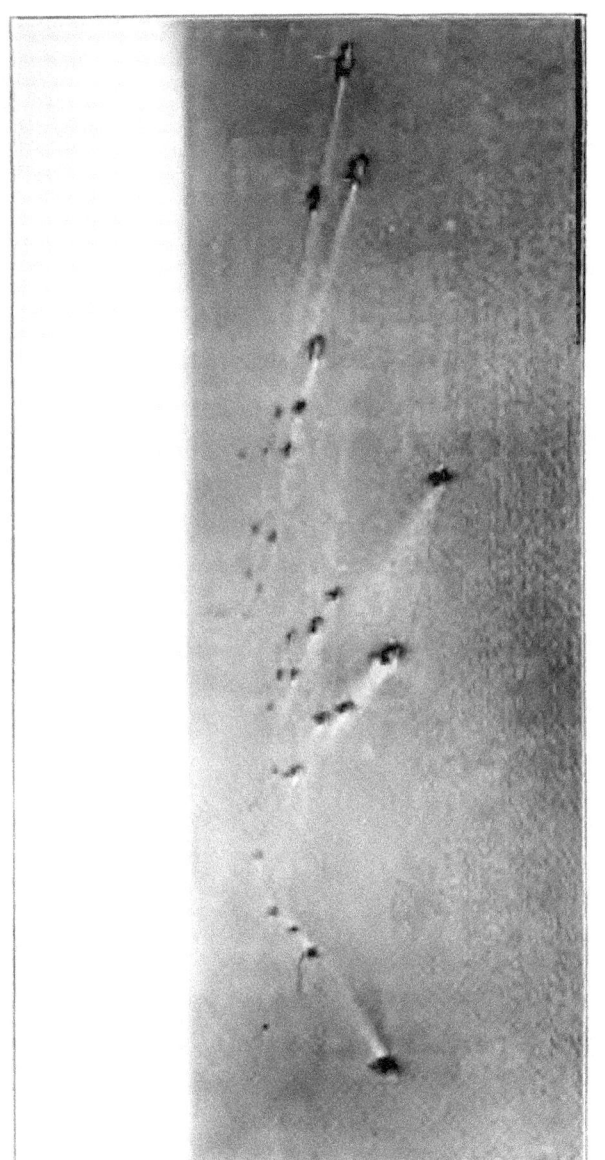

A convoy approaching its haven of safety in European waters.

date. In fact, all sorts of inventions and plans for unsinkable ships, and for the destruction of submarines were being received by the Admiralty and by the Navy Department, and some of these were excellent in principle. But it was not wise to take these too seriously for the present, because of the time necessary for their institution. The situation called for a remedy, the necessary component parts of which were already in the hands of the authorities and available for immediate use; that is, what the advent of the American destroyers afforded—the necessary number of destroyers for convoy—and with their arrival the system could be immediately established.

CHAPTER 3

The Establishment of Bases

It has already been said that from June to September, 1917, would be the critical period of the submarine war; there was also a critical area, and this was in the waters between the Southwestern coast of Ireland and Cape Finisterre, or Brest, France. All ships from the United States, Canada, South America, the Mediterranean, and Africa, had to pass through this area to get into the Southern and Western ports of England, such as Southampton, Plymouth, Cardiff, Holyhead, or Liverpool. A considerable portion of shipping from the United States and Canada, was directed to pass to the North of Ireland, to Glasgow and Liverpool, thereby avoiding the necessity of steaming into this "neck of a bottle" formed by the coast lines of England and France.

But this did not seriously relieve the congestion of traffic; in fact, the congestion could not be relieved. In order to escort safely the hundreds of vessels which passed through this critical area South of Ireland, escorts to the convoys had to be provided. This meant that any location suitable for a base on the South coast of Ireland, would be very desirable, and Queenstown was the first locality chosen as an American Naval base. It formed a halfway point between the Western ports of England, and the rendezvous at sea between which the convoys would be escorted.

★★★★★★★★★

The rendezvous at sea was the position at which destroyers would meet a group of merchant vessels from North and South America: this position was generally some 200 or 300 miles west of the British Isles and France.

★★★★★★★★★★

The next base to be decided upon was Brest, the location of which afforded many of the same advantages as those of Queenstown; both were located at the approach to the chief European ports.

The first flotilla of American destroyers ordered to Europe was sent directly to Queenstown. This detachment, consisting of six vessels under Commander Taussig, U. S. N., steamed into Queenstown harbour at noon on April 26, 1917. The British Naval personnel at Queenstown knew that these vessels were coming, and were expecting them sometime during the day, but hardly expected that they would arrive at noon, the hour which Taussig had designated by wireless, because of the delays and uncertainties involved in a trip across the Atlantic.

But surely enough they did, and at a few minutes before noon, smoke was seen on the Western horizon, and then one, two, three, four, five, six little specks came up out of the ocean. Two mine sweepers were immediately sent out a few miles to sweep a channel clear for them, for who knew but that a German submarine might have laid mines at the entrance to the harbour during the previous night. Great were the cheers from all at the base, for these vessels were coming to help in the war against the submarine at a time when the need for destroyers was very great.

As they steamed up the harbour, few, perhaps, realised what the advent of these American vessels really meant. It meant that America and England, sister nations, had at last joined hands against their common enemy. In memory of this day, it will be for the welfare of America to forget what her children are taught in school books about English tyranny; and it will be for the welfare of Great Britain to remember that, though separated by three thousand miles of water, she has a friend who helped her in a great struggle. These thoughts, shared as they are today by many Anglo-Saxons, were beautifully expressed to Admiral Sims before his departure from England in a picture given to him.

The picture is entitled, "The Return of the *Mayflower*"; in the foreground is the *Mayflower*, as that vessel probably appeared—behind it a full-fledged squadron of American destroyers as they appeared that morning entering Queenstown harbour. Previous to the arrival of the American destroyers, Admiral Sims had decided to commence his policy of supplementing the weaker portions of the Royal Navy by handing the operating command of these vessels over to Vice-Admiral Sir Lewis Bayly, R. N., the Commander in Chief of the Southwest coast of Ireland. In this way, Admiral Sims showed himself not only the first great Allied chief to propose unity of command, but also the first to put such doctrines into effect.

He was still to have administrative command over these vessels, but as far as operations were concerned, they were to serve with the British forces under Admiral Bayly. In order to ensure harmony between these forces of two different nations, Vice-Admiral Bayly appointed Captain J. R. P. Pringle, U. S. N., who was Admiral Sims' Chief of Staff at Queenstown, as his first assistant. Vice-Admiral Bayly sent these vessels as they steamed up the harbour, the heartiest welcome and congratulations upon their arrival in European waters; in concluding this message, he informed Commander Taussig that all facilities at his base were at the disposal of the American vessels, and asked what repair work was necessary and how long before the American flotilla would be ready for duty.

Commander Taussig's reply was prompt, and read, "As soon as we refuel, Sir." Such an answer, after a hard trip across the Atlantic, from a destroyer's officer, whose vessels were never intended to cross the ocean except in emergencies, gave the American vessels a wonderful place—a very extraordinary place in fact—in the esteem of the authorities of the Royal Navy. The tale of Commander Taussig's reply soon spread broadcast, and as late as February, 1919, it was still being told at the English dinner table as a remarkable accomplishment.

That is what it was, and it immediately convinced the officers of the English navy that the types of vessels and men aboard the American vessels were of the very highest order. Whatever the accomplishments of the American Navy had been in the past, all these were temporarily eclipsed by this incident. The American crews were allowed four days' rest before commencing their new tasks as a belligerent Allied Navy.

The American destroyers, in that another twenty-five or thirty would soon join them at Queenstown, were confronted with the problem of enlarging the scope of the facilities and requirements necessary at a naval base. Queenstown had been used as a base by the British, but the present and future influx of twenty or thirty more vessels, made vast expansion necessary. Admiral Sims had already laid down the law that all vessels at U. S. Naval bases in European waters should be self-maintaining, which meant in the case of Queenstown, that many store-houses, barracks, hospitals, recreation rooms, and repair facilities had to be provided.

Work was commenced almost immediately on the construction of such buildings, and the growth of the base was rapid. In undertakings of this sort, as was the case wherever the British Naval Authorities were encountered, the members of the Royal Navy left no stone upturned in offering every assistance possible, a courtesy which will always be remembered by those who served at Queenstown.

The most important facility necessary at Queenstown was an organisation capable of executing rapid and extensive repairs. Destroyers always have needed, and always will need, a great deal of watching and repairing. The English dockyards were already so overcrowded that any repair work which could be done at the base would save time and trouble, for, besides not being a burden to the dock yards, the efficient upkeep of a vessel would be of value in keeping that vessel in the running. To serve this purpose two mother ships, the U. S. S. *Dixie* and the U. S. S. *Melville*, (Admiral Sims' flagship in Europe), to be used as store and repair ships, were sent to Queenstown.

The record which these two ships established in keeping the destroyers in good repair, probably contributed more to the efficient upkeep of the destroyers than any one thing. Whenever a destroyer returned to port after several days at sea with convoys, she would send a message to the *Melville* stating what repairs would be necessary, and by the time that the destroyer had made fast to her buoy, a working party from the *Melville* would be ready to commence work at once. The greater portion of repair work was done by the crew of the *Melville* rather than by those of the destroyers, for the duty at sea was so arduous that all time in port was needed for rest.

There was no task short of a lost propeller or a severely injured turbine that the men from the *Melville* could not handle. In the general scheme of operations, it was planned that each destroyer should have four days' duty at sea and two days in port, which meant that each vessel would be on duty 67% of the time; statistics of operations show that the average time at sea for all destroyers was about 66%. This splendid record was largely the result of the efficient and excellent work performed by the repair ships and their crews.

But before the Americans felt themselves fully established, they joined in the work of the British. Vice-Admiral Bayly, R. N., who was a veritable horse for work, and Captain J. R. P. Pringle, U. S. N., Admiral Sims' Chief of Staff at Queenstown, rightly believed that, as long as there was a war in progress, the idleness of any vessel was a military crime. When any occasion arose in which a destroyer was ready for duty but was awaiting the approach of a convoy or a similar assignment of duty, that vessel was not allowed to stay idle, but was immediately sent out on patrol duty of some sort.

The actual escort of a convoy was an arduous task. Four or five or more destroyers would leave Queenstown and proceed westward to

The U. S. S. Duncan and the H. M. S. Wizard. Notice the difference in construction. A dispute once arose between Admiral Sims and some British officers as to the relative merits of English and American destroyers. An English officer said that the British destroyers were better because they were more manly and sturdy, and that though American vessels were the more graceful, they looked effeminate. Admiral Sims replied: "The female is the more deadly of the species."

pick up a convoy about 200 miles West of Ireland.

They would then escort this convoy to Liverpool or some other port, and then turn around and escort an outward-bound convoy to a point some 200 miles West of Ireland. Here they would pick up another incoming convoy and take it to a Western English port, or, if they were lucky, be relieved by another detachment of destroyers as they passed near Queenstown. A slow convoy would necessitate many inconceivable forms of antics and exercises in the execution of proper vigilance. A fast convoy would call for the same vigilance, but would be a great deal more severe on the destroyers and their personnel than a slow one. A few hours with a 20-knot convoy, which meant that the destroyers must maintain a speed of 23 knots at least, or the experience of two or three days of heavy storms, imposed as severe a strain upon the human body and nerve power as has been experienced in this war. The strain upon the ships themselves was often far greater than their designers expected them to weather.

If the reader desires to learn of the romance of convoy duty, I can only refer him to some of the excellent books of Lieutenant Freeman, R. N. on that subject, or, better still, let the reader himself inquire into the thoughts of the seaman who was ordered aloft at two a. m. to the lookout nest on the forward mast of a destroyer, which was rolling forty-five degrees on a dark and stormy night, and making twenty knots; or ask the young regular or reserve officer what thoughts went through his mind, when he was aroused from lifeless slumbers to go on watch for four hours as officer of the deck of his destroyer, awakened by a touch from the quartermaster and these cheering words: "11.45, Sir, and Mr. Smith says it is cold and wet, Sir;" and whatever there was of a romantic or human side in this war, will be found.

A brief statistical *resumé* shows that during the ten and a half months of 1918 the Queenstown destroyers escorted 39% of all the traffic passing in and out by way of the South coast of Ireland.

★★★★★★★★★★

In May, 1918, there were 33 American destroyers at Queenstown. Twelve of these the following month were transferred to Brest. As new destroyers came over, they were sent to Queenstown, and a corresponding number already at Queenstown were ordered to Brest. In Sept., 1918, 36 chasers arrived at Queenstown: they carried out some excellent operations, but their activities were cut short by the Armistice.

★★★★★★★★★★

The crew of the U. 58 surrendering to the U. S. S. Fanning and Nicholson.

In July and August alone, they escorted a total of 2,340,000 tons without a single casualty to any convoy; in other words, they escorted about one-sixth of the shipping afloat on the high seas of the world, without a single loss.

The experiences of the American destroyers at Queenstown calling for the greatest interest are those of the sinking of a submarine by the U. S. S. *Fanning* and *Nicholson* on November 17, 1917, and the loss of the U. S. S. *Jacob Jones* on November 5th of the same year. The *Fanning* and *Nicholson* were escorting a convoy, when a submarine was sighted. They ran towards it at full speed and dropped depth charges over the spot beneath which it had submerged, and then circled around the vicinity while the submarine rose to the surface only to submerge again in a moment. Once more they dropped depth charges, one of which injured the elevation apparatus, corresponding to a rudder of the submarine.

The submarine sank to a great depth, after which a commanding officer blew his tanks, bringing the vessel to the surface. The *Fanning* immediately opened fire, and a moment later the crew came up on deck through the conning tower and surrendered. This was the first "prize" of the American Navy in Europe, and, as will be remembered, the news was heralded with enthusiasm in this country. The submarine was the *U-58*.

On November 5, 1917, the U. S. S. *Jacob Jones*, one of our newest and best destroyers, was steaming alone not far from the Scilly islands. Late in the afternoon she was struck by a torpedo from an enemy submarine and sank in a few minutes, a little over half of her crew being saved. The wireless of the *Jacob Jones* was put out of commission by the explosion, but later the commander-in-chief on the South coast of Ireland, Admiral Bayly, received a wireless announcing that the *Jacob Jones* had sunk at a certain time, in a given latitude, and that the survivors were in the boats and on rafts; help was requested. This was a curious situation, and there is no doubt in the minds of the officers stationed at Queenstown but that wireless was sent by the German submarine.

Among the requisites of a Naval Base are recreation centres. There are no greater believers in the value of suitable rest and recreation for crews than Admiral Sims and his associates, who were determined that the Queenstown Forces should enjoy their moments ashore, and saw to it that they did. A "Men's Club," in which almost nightly little amateur theatricals, dances, or "movies" were given by the crews of the vessels in port, was the centre of these attractions. The necessity for this sort of thing was more clearly realised after a few unfortunate disturbances between the sailors and the Irish at Cork. The Southern Irishman did not seem an easy person with whom to get along, and no doubt the apparent prosperity of the American sailors rubbed him a bit the wrong way.

This, coupled with the attitude of many of the Irish towards the war, probably established the grounds for bad feeling. In other words, these affairs resulted from a misunderstanding between the sailors and the Irishmen, the latter of whom are suffering because the force which controls them—and this force is not the British Government— does not offer them the benefits of education, at least in our American sense. Their reoccurrence was prevented when all shore leave to Cork was denied the American sailors, and from then on, the "Men's Club" and other recreation centres were of great value.

The leaders of the various armies and navies in this war were concerned over the matter of cooperation, the success or failure of which rested on their shoulders. However, the attainment of understanding between the rank and file of the different forces was also to be considered, and this was a delicate problem to handle. In looking over the unwritten history of Queenstown and in talks with American officers and men who served there, the impression is gathered immediately that the best of feeling existed between the personnel of the American and British Navies. This unity of sentiment and effort began with Admiral Bayly and Admiral Sims and was disseminated right down through the officers of lesser rank and the enlisted men.

A good example of it is seen in the fact that when British and American destroyers were at sea together, either a British or an American would be the senior officer present; sometimes an American officer would command the unit and at other times a British officer. But in spite of the efforts of the officers, arguments, relieved by brawls, arose between the enlisted men. This was really only natural, for an Englishman is a "Limy" and an American is a "Yank" and there is enough of a difference to keep time from hanging too heavy.

★★★★★★★★★★

For some unknown reason, the British during this war, and in the past, have been called "Limies," which is short for "Limejuicers." I do not know what the origin of the term is, but it might well be reversed now.

★★★★★★★★★★

From my own experience as a "gob" in England, I know that these

33

occasional disturbances were not the result of any deep feeling. The Englishman is a very conservative person, who too often gives the impression that he is holding aloof; the American, on the other hand, is very frank and talkative and apparently wishes to shake hands with the world when he is out of his own country. When this indifference of the Englishman, which was often taken for conceit, came into contact with the enthusiasm of his cousin from over the water, who often was vivacious in relating "how we do things in America," action followed.

Thus, one hears the statement that the Americans fought with the British more than with the Frenchman, an explanation of which is simple. The American is different from both the Britisher and the Frenchman; he cannot argue with the Frenchman but he can argue with the Englishmen; and an argument was usually the training camp for a good old-fashioned fight.

In order to show how little gaps of sentiment arising from these disturbances were bridged over, I mention here a periodical of satire and humour which would occasionally appear for sale at the Base. This little paper went a long way towards keeping down the differences which arose as a result of the conflicting nationalities and from allowing the men to take such matters too seriously. As an illustration of its contents, I am giving a resume of one of the articles; it may not be correct in detail, but the ideas expressed in it are to the point.

The article recorded the preliminary proceedings of an imaginary board of investigation held to inquire into the complaints of a British destroyer officer, that the commanding officer of an American destroyer had "messed" fifteen minutes earlier on his vessel than the British officer on his. The chairman of the board was purported as being Captain Pringle, the American chief of staff. The investigation opened with each officer explaining his case; in a few minutes the argument became heated; and the conflicting use of American and British slang was prominent.

Captain Pringle arose and requested that the English officers speak in the English language; this remark immediately called an Englishman to his feet, who claimed that the English language originated in England; this statement in turn produced another argument as to who knew the most about the English language, the Americans or the Englishmen. This continued for some minutes, until a British officer told an American to close his "blinking trap." Captain Pringle immediately jumped to his feet and said the meeting should proceed no further until the meaning of the term "blinking trap" had been explained.

Dictionaries, naval regulations, convoy orders, almanacks, and similar stores of information were all consulted, but no enlightenment was offered upon the term "blinking trap."

After an hour of this important research work, Captain Pringle said he was going to have some lunch, whereupon a Britisher objected, saying that such discourtesy, as that exhibited by Captain Pringle, was unprecedented in the history of his—the British officer's—family. The meeting adjourned by Captain Pringle expressing himself strongly in doubt as to whether the British officer ever had a family.

But other than occasional brawls, the general feeling between the crews of the vessels of the two nations was excellent, and I have no hesitancy in saying that I know that those Americans and Britishers who took pains to learn the other fellow's point of view came out of this war—and certainly home from Queenstown—with admiration for the people, the ideals and accomplishments of the other fellow's nation.

BREST

During the early part of the nineteenth century and in the preceding century, Brest had been a seaport and naval centre of great importance; in the first three years of this war, it had played but a small part. In June, 1917, a Fleet of American yachts, transformed into warships, left this country, and, stopping at the Bermudas and Azores, arrived at Brest at the end of the month. These ships were dispatched to Europe in answer to Admiral Sims' urgent call for anti-submarine craft, a fuller discussion of which follows later. They were to a large extent manned by young naval reserve volunteers, most of whose sea experiences had been limited to the bathing beach; nevertheless, they were the first American war vessels to reach the coast of France.

Their crews were an eager and very enthusiastic aggregation, many of them college men; one of the vessels, the U. S. S. *Harvard*, was almost completely manned by undergraduates of Harvard—the classes of 1918 and 1919. It seems curious, that after the American Navy had been training some 80,000 men for years and years, with the advent of war, the Navy Department should have sent the recruits of the Reserve Force among the first to Europe.

Perhaps the department realised how excellent their services would be in spite of their lack of training, and the least that can be said of them is that their services were excellent, for no crew of greater "land lubbers" ever set sail—still less to go to war—aboard any ship; and yet

35

A convoy entering Brest. The chill of French fogs and rain will never be forgotten by those who braved the elements for eighteen months.

no crews ever acquitted themselves more creditably.

The yachts commenced their duties shortly after their arrival. At Queenstown there already was a naval base; at Brest there was a French naval base, but as France was not a first-class naval power, many of those facilities and necessities which go to make up an efficient base, were lacking. This was partly the result of the decadence of Brest as a naval port of first importance, and partly due to the fact that in 1914, at the outbreak of the war, Great Britain had informed France that she herself would try to handle whatever naval situations might arise. This left France free to devote her entire energy to the development of her army, and relieved her of the necessity of expanding her navy, the greater part of which, because of the easy protection of the French coasts by the Royal Navy, had been transferred to the Mediterranean. Thus, when the American yachts arrived at Brest, they found their new home lacking the design of the Brooklyn Navy Yard.

For three months the yachts, under Captain Fletcher, U. S. N., were the only American warships at Brest, during which time the work of preparing the base to serve as a port of debarkation for American troops and supplies and as a home for American warships in the future was carried on. The yachts were employed in convoy duty; the larger and faster ones, such as the *Noma*, were used in deep-sea escorts, while the others were dispatched up and down the coast from Brest to Bordeaux and intermediate ports. During this period of evolution, for that is what it was, the U. S. S. *Alcedo* was torpedoed and sunk; its loss was the first serious casualty to the American Navy in Europe.

Admiral Sims always realised that the Western coast of France would eventually be the chief area of activity of the American Navy; therefore, as more destroyers came over, they were ordered to Brest. Later as the influx of American troops and supplies grew, he designated Lorient, St. Nazaire, Rochefort, and Bordeaux as bases, and assigned vessels to them. In October 1917, he ordered Rear-Admiral Wilson, who had been in command of the U. S. Naval Forces at Gibraltar, to Brest and appointed him Commander of our Naval Forces in France. Admiral Wilson was in command of his forces from both an operative and administrative point of view: in both he was directly responsible to Admiral Sims in London.

When Brest first began to function as a real base, the duty of the yachts, as has already been mentioned, was that of escorting coastal convoys. As the influx of American troops grew, it became very evident that anti-submarine vessels with a greater cruising radius and

U. S. S. Leviathan

The H. M. S. Mauretania and U. S. S. Leviathan, two transports
which carried eight or nine thousand troops to France per trip.

higher speed were needed. The remark was once made that these yachts were fast enough on a downhill stretch, but not on the level. They could handle the coastal convoys up and down the coast but could not escort them 200 miles out in the Atlantic; until the Fall of 1917 the British destroyers at Plymouth and the American destroyers at Queenstown had shouldered this duty.

As the volume of traffic increased it became too much for them; consequently, the additional destroyers were stationed at Brest. After their arrival two sorts of convoy duty were adopted: the deep-sea convoy duty and the coastal convoys. In the former, the destroyers would proceed to sea, pick up an incoming convoy, escort it to the coast, and there be met by the yachts and gunboats, which in turn would escort the various vessels to their port of destination. After January, 1918, the base and its duties grew rapidly, and we find that during the months of 1918 these Forces escorted 91% of all the convoys in and out of France, or about 1,700,000 tons per month. In November, 1918, 78 vessels and 12,000 men were stationed at Brest. (These figures include the crews of those ships and the men stationed along the Western coast of France, at Lorient, St. Nazaire, Rochefort, and Bordeaux, and at the Naval Aviation bases.)

The Forces at Brest made their "first kill" on May 21, 1919. The *Christabel*, a former yacht, was escorting the merchant ship *Deanœ*, when a periscope was sighted between the yacht and the ship. The *Christabel* stood in towards the estimated position of the submarine, dropped a depth charge; and a few minutes later another. After the second one had exploded, a third explosion, under water, followed. The second depth charge had injured the submarine, which was of the minelaying type, and this had caused the third explosion. This boat was the *UC-56*. The following morning it put into Santander, on the North coast of Spain, and because of injuries received, was forced to intern.

On August 8, 1918, the U. S. S. *Tucker*, one of our best destroyers, sighted a submarine while 150 miles Southwest of Brest. The submarine was first seen when it suddenly came to the surface within 200 yards of the *Tucker*. The *Tucker* immediately opened fire with her forward gun, and at full speed, ran towards it to attack it with depth charges. The submarine immediately submerged. The destroyer then passed over to the spot where the submarine had submerged, dropped several depth charges, and described a circle in order to pass over the same spot again. While the *Tucker* was thus manoeuvring, the subma-

© Underwood & Underwood

The German Submarine U. C. 56 interned at Santandu, Spain, as a result of injuries received in an engagement with the U. S. S. "Christabel."

rine came to the surface again and the *Tucker* opened fire, one of the shells apparently hitting it. Again, the submarine submerged and the *Tucker* passed over the spot dropping depth charges. A few moments later the bow of the submarine appeared above the waves, at an angle which indicated that all was not well on board, and then slowly sank.

The commanding officer, in handing in his report of this encounter, felt convinced that a submarine had been destroyed. In consulting the charts of submarine movements, which I shall fully discuss later, it would appear that there was no submarine within 100 miles of the locality in which the attack took place. It remains unknown to this day whether this submarine was sunk or not, for no further evidences of her operations were noted, and no previous evidence of her presence had been observed.

★★★★★★★★★★

It is difficult to say there was no submarine present, for all hands claimed to have seen it. On the other hand, every submarine in existence could be accounted for, and this one seen by the *Tucker* was not included in current intelligence. The matter is still unsolved, and probably will remain so, though official credit for its destruction was given to the *Tucker*.

★★★★★★★★★★

Keen rivalry soon grew up between the Queenstown and the Brest destroyers, and it was expressed in many ways. The chief "bone" of contention was as to which base was doing the hardest work, that is, handling the greatest volume of traffic in proportion to the number of destroyers available. Statistics show that the Queenstown boats had a little the better of the argument. The Queenstown officer used to tell, and will tell today, the tale that whenever his ship put into Brest, most of the Brest destroyers were in the harbour; on the other hand, the Brest officers will tell that the Queenstown vessels were always going to Liverpool so that the officers and crew could get a couple of days' leave to London.

This rivalry, of course, was a splendid thing and it made for *esprit de corps*, a necessity to all great undertakings. And that is what these operations were. The figures I have quoted, showing the volume of traffic escorted, do not really convey the right impression as to the amount of work accomplished and the hardships endured. Life on a destroyer, at best, is not pleasant, and if we consider that all of these destroyers were out in all sorts of weather for four days out of every six, a better idea of the service they rendered will be gained.

An American destroyer escorting a convoy. Smoke screens proved effective when wind conditions were right.

The manner in which Admiral Wilson cooperated with the French was most commendable. Capt. R. H. Jackson, U. S. N., was ordered to Paris where he was given a position in the French Ministry of Marine. Brest, with its historic background and picturesque surroundings, as the chief city of quaint old Brittany, was the subject of much interest, and later many literary efforts of our men. The geniality of the French aristocrat, or peasant, will undoubtedly always be remembered by those who learned to know and appreciate the pleasures and comforts of the "old world" civilization.

GIBRALTAR

It has already been said that Queenstown and Brest were chosen as suitable locations for American Naval bases because they were situated at the gateway to the British Isles and France; there was one other gateway to European waters, and that was Gibraltar. Here Admiral Sims established a third base. On August 18, 1918, the U. S. S. *Birmingham*, a scout cruiser and the flag ship of the patrol force of the U. S. Atlantic fleet, steamed into Gibraltar. On August 20, Admiral Sims sent Admiral Wilson, (ordered to command forces at Brest in October, 1917), whose flag the *Birmingham* was flying, a cable instructing him to cooperate in every way with the British Forces at Gibraltar.

Admiral Wilson showed his comprehension of this policy by dispatching the U. S. S. *Sacramento* as escort to an English convoy on August 22. On the other hand, Rear-Admiral Grant, R. N., showed his willingness to help the United States Naval Forces by offering them the use of their supplies of all kinds: food, fuel, coal, and repair facilities. Thus began the activities of the United States Navy in the Mediterranean in August, 1917.

The duties of the American vessels varied greatly, mainly because of the variety of the types of vessels. These consisted of cruisers, destroyers, gunboats, coastguard cutters, and yachts converted into warships. The larger vessels, cruisers, destroyers and coastguard cutters, were continually on duty at sea with convoys between Gibraltar and England, or between many points in the Mediterranean. They also escorted large merchant convoys bound to and from the United States or South American ports. In this duty, it was not unusual for a vessel to be absent at sea for ten days or two weeks and then to return to port, only to be dispatched again in three or four days on similar duty.

The smaller craft, that is, gunboats and yachts, came in for their share of hard work, by serving as escorts to many local Mediterranean convoys and to those bound for the Azores. Their task was perhaps more difficult than that of the larger vessels, in that they were less seaworthy, while the yachts were never designed to serve as war vessels. Patrol duty formed no small part of their curriculum, as a constant watch at the mouth of the Mediterranean was always kept. Their work was at all times satisfactory and they fulfilled the demands made upon them, a result rendered possible only by their efficient upkeep.

The volume of work actually done by the American vessels at Gibraltar is shown by a few figures. During July and August, 1918, for instance, the average time at sea for all the vessels was 57%. This means roughly that each ship was at sea six days out of ten; of the four days in port, at least two, or perhaps three, were essential for repairs, refuelling, taking on provisions, etc. During these two months they steamed 170,000 miles, or six times around the world, and were at sea about 17,000 hours. They furnished 25% of the escorts for local Mediterranean convoys, and over 75% of the escorts for the ocean and deep-sea convoys.

In the offensive war against the submarine, they played their part and suffered their losses. The action of the U. S. S. *Lydonia*, a yacht which had assumed a belligerent aspect, stands out conspicuously. On May 11, while she was proceeding as an escort, along with British warships, to a convoy of merchant vessels in the Mediterranean, a submarine was sighted. It appeared that the submarine was manoeuvring to get into position to fire a torpedo, but by the skilful cooperation of H. M. S. *Basilisk* and the U. S. S. *Lydonia*, a network of depth charges was laid around the submarine. The submarine was not seen again; three months later it was discovered she had been sunk.

The loss of the U. S. S. *Tampa*, a former coastguard vessel, is one of the greatest tragedies and mysteries of the sea in the history of the war. On September 26, she was proceeding with an English convoy from Gibraltar to Milford Haven. When in sight of the English coast, she detached herself from the convoy and stood in towards the coast. She was sighted from some of the shore stations for a few moments; a slight mist then descended and hid her from view. A loud explosion was heard, and the *Tampa* was never seen again. American destroyers searched the area for two days in the hope of finding some survivors, but the only traces found were the floating body of an American sailor and some wreckage marked *Tampa*.

★★★★★★★★★★

The cause of the destruction of the *Tampa* is unknown. There was no evidence to show that a submarine was the cause of the disaster, for no submarine was in the vicinity. It is possible that she struck a floating mine, but more probable, that an internal explosion took place. That something had gone wrong on board can be surmised by the manner in which she detached herself from the convoy without orders to do so.

★★★★★★★★★★

The incident which perhaps stands out above all other experiences of the United States Navy in European Waters is that of the U. S. S. *Senaca*, another coastguard ship based at Gibraltar. On September 16, 1918, she was proceeding from England to Gibraltar with a convoy when the British ship *Wellington* was struck by a torpedo. The *Senaca*, under Lieutenant-Commander Wheeler, dropped enough depth charges in the direction whence the torpedo came to prevent the submarine from attempting more damage. Shortly after the *Wellington* was torpedoed, her merchant crew deserted her and came alongside the *Senaca* in their boats. The master of the *Wellington* told Commander Wheeler that with the help of about thirty men, he thought the *Wellington* could be kept afloat until she reached port.

Ten of the *Wellington's* crew volunteered to go back to try to save the ship; about 35 refused. Lieutenant Brown of the *Senaca* asked permission to go with the master of the *Wellington* and picked 16 of the crew to help him. The *Senaca*, in the meantime, was ordered to proceed with the remainder of the convoy and so left her seventeen volunteers to be of what service they could. It seemed that they would be able to keep the *Wellington* afloat, but a heavy wind and sea made their task impossible.

An S. O. S. call was sent out and answered by the U. S. S. *Warrington*, a destroyer based at Brest. The *Warrington* came to the rescue at full speed and arrived at the scene a few minutes before the *Wellington* sank. In the heavy seas and the unusually dark night the task of rescuing the men was difficult. Eight of the *Senaca's* crew and Lt. Brown were rescued, but ten went down with the ship they had volunteered to save.

The co-operation which existed between the Americans and British was not so noticeable among the French and Italians. Later it was established, but for several months, convoys were escorted by the vessels of two or three nations, and the misunderstandings which thereby arose were sometimes disastrous and occasionally humorous. I remember that the captain of one of our vessels who apparently had a grudge against somebody once sent in a report like this:

A——— destroyer then got excited and opened fire in various directions. (Nationality of the destroyer here omitted for obvious reasons). The first shot missed my bows by a few feet, the second one carried away a stack of a——— destroyer; the third sank a cargo ship loaded with rum. I think greater cooperation is necessary.

CHAPTER 4

Progress

After the American Naval Bases at Queenstown, Brest, and Gibraltar had been established, each one of which was located along a gateway to Allied European ports, it may be said that the American Navy was effectively participating in the war. It must be remembered that the establishment of Queenstown as a base and the full growth of Brest as a base were separated by six months' time; thus, one must not become confused and think that the matter already dealt with has been discussed in mere chronological order.

By August and September, 1917, the convoy had been introduced and put into operation. What an enormous piece of work this entailed and what minute detail the execution of such a system required is too long a story to deal with here. Its effective organisation was the result of the wholehearted cooperation between the different shipping organisations and the British and American Navies, the American end of which was so ably organised by Commander Babcock, U. S. N., and later handled by Captain Byron A. Long, U. S. N. at Admiral Sims' headquarters. It is sufficient to say that in order to make the convoy system practical and successful, every Allied ship afloat had to be provided with copious instructions and convoy orders, many codes, and a great volume of other information such as sailing orders, shipping routes, etc.

The actual working of a convoy is an interesting study. Twenty or thirty ships would meet together off the American coast and proceed Eastward under the escort of a cruiser.

★★★★★★★★

A cruiser was dispatched with the convoys as a protective unit against enemy commerce raiders; against a submarine they were not capable of assuming an offensive role, such as destroyers.

★★★★★★★★

When about 200 miles from the coasts of Ireland or France, at a given date, hour, or position, these ships would be met by a variable number of destroyers, and ensemble the great procession Eastward would continue. A zigzag course was usually commenced at dawn and continued throughout the day unless foggy or stormy. It was not usually employed at night because the darkness made its use unnecessary, though such ships as the *Leviathan, Aquitania, Olympic,* whose enormous hulls above the water were visible even at night, usually continued their zigzag at all times. The virtue of a zigzag course lay in the fact that a submarine would experience great difficulty in determining the course and speed of a ship or convoy whose course was irregular.

A torpedo, to be accurate, practically had to be fired from a distance of under 1000 yards; when a ship or convoy was steering a zigzag course it was very difficult for the submarine to estimate the ships' probable position a few moments later. An interesting example of the effectiveness of the zigzag is seen in the case of the *Olympic,* on May 12, 1918. The *Olympic,* loaded with American troops, was proceeding Eastward, about 150 miles off Brest, escorted by American destroyers. An enemy submarine, the *U-103,* at dawn saw her approaching and manoeuvred to get into position to fire a torpedo. The submarine attempted to estimate the course and speed of the *Olympic,* which was steering a zigzag course, and submerged to approach closer to her prey.

A few moments later the commanding officer and the crew of the submarine were surprised by a terrific crash against the hull of their vessel; water began to pour in. One of the *Olympic's* propellers had crashed through the hull. The tanks of the submarine were blown, thereby bringing it to the surface, and the entire crew called for help as they deserted the sinking boat. ("Tanks blown" means buoyancy tanks emptied of water.) The survivors were rescued by the U. S. S. *Davis.* The calculations of the commanding officer of the submarine had been upset by the *Olympic's* vicious zigzag and speed, and he paid for his mistake by the loss of his vessel.

To return to the study of the convoy. Imagine thirty great ships all huddled together changing their courses every few minutes, and then imagine what havoc might be wrought if one ship made a mistake. Mistakes were made and havoc was wrought, but as time went on, the mistakes grew less, but were always to be guarded against.

★★★★★★★★★★

On October 9, 1918, the U. S. S. *Shaw,* a Queenstown destroyer, was proceeding towards Southampton accompanying the H. M. S. *Aqui-*

The U. S. S. Shaw in rough weather, and the same
ship after her collision with the Aquitania in
October, 1918.

tania, which was carrying American troops; both vessels were maintaining a speed of 23 knots. The *Shaw* was about 250 yards away from the big vessel and running parallel to her when her rudder "jammed" and she turned towards the *Aquitania*. Her commanding officer appreciated the situation in a moment and realised that if he reversed his engines and tried to stop his vessel the sharp bows of the *Shaw* would pierce the hull of the *Aquitania* and perhaps sink it, and that if he continued in the course forced upon him by the jamming of his rudder, the *Aquitania* would ram him as he crossed her bows.

Not wishing to sink six thousand troops, he took the latter course and allowed the *Aquitania* to run into him. In this collision the *Aquitania* practically cut the *Shaw* in half, and several of the crew and officers were drowned. For this action Commander William Glassford of the *Shaw* was very highly commended by Admiral Sims and the British Admiralty; for though he wrecked his own vessel, he did it in such a way that six thousand lives were made safe, at the risk of his own.

★★★★★★★★★★

In the meantime, destroyers would proceed at a speed slightly greater than that of the convoy in order to search the area through which the convoy was passing. Two destroyers, three or four miles ahead of the main body of the convoy, would steam back and forth across the path of the approaching vessels, eagerly searching for any signs of a lurking enemy. A destroyer on each flank would run in towards the convoy and then out a mile or so from it and then perhaps fall back a bit to cover the port or starboard quarter, or, unless there were another destroyer covering the rear, fall behind the convoy and protect it from a submarine which might be following the procession.

Suddenly one destroyer might see some disturbance in the water. Up would go the submarine warning signal, the convoy would turn sharply to left or right, as ordered, and the destroyers would drop depth charges and hang around for an hour or so to see if the submarine might reappear. When a ship was torpedoed in a convoy, under no circumstances were the other ships of the convoy allowed to stop and offer assistance; to do so would only invite further mischief from the submarine. The one or two destroyers would offer all the assistance necessary, while the convoy fled from the location of the disaster. Also, when a submarine was sighted, the merchant ships or troop transports under escort of destroyers were never allowed to take part in the attack upon the submarine.

The destroyers were the offensive and defensive weapons of a convoy, while a transport's or merchant ship's guns were for protection

A troop convoy entering Brest. Note the sign at the base of the gun, "No Troops Allowed." If any man, sailor or soldier, had tried to do half of the things he was forbidden to do, on a Transport, he probably would have died from exhaustion.

only in an attack in which no escorts were present. On one occasion, the *Leviathan*, May 31, 1918, when off Brest, sighted what her officers believed to be a submarine, and this great ship, with her eight six-inch guns, immediately opened fire, thereby rendering the protection which the destroyers afforded absolutely useless. In this case, the officers of the destroyers from Brest recognised the disturbance as a well-known tide-rip and hence were not really hampered; but, if a submarine had been the cause of the disturbance in the water, the *Leviathan* would have been open to attack. How could the destroyers have dropped depth charges over the disturbance in the water if the *Leviathan* was firing at that spot?

The convoy system during these first few months of trial proved successful, that is, its introduction reduced the sinkings by more than 50%; but very nearly 400,000 tons per month were still being destroyed. These losses outweighed by far the new construction. As long as this condition existed, the Allies were on the losing end of the game; and further efforts were necessary to improve matters. It was realised that this would be a very long and hard task and that the results from any improvements would not happen overnight. There were two ways of improving the situation; first, by centralising the control of the management and routing and shipping, and secondly, by increasing the number of anti-submarine vessels.

Soon after the introduction of the convoy system, the necessity of cooperation and speed in the handling of shipping became very apparent. If twenty ships were to sail from Hampton Roads, it was of vital importance to have every one of those ships ready to sail on time, and thereby avoid delay. The time in which an average cargo ship made a "turnaround," that is, left one port, crossed the ocean, discharged her cargo, returned, and was ready to leave again, was about two months. This meant that such a ship could make six round trips a year, barring time lost in repairs.

If the time for loading and unloading, and the trips at sea, could all be reduced so as to make it possible for the ship to make a "turnaround" in six weeks, twelve weeks a year, or three months, would be saved; and twelve weeks saved would mean two extra trips a year, or an increase of 33% in the cargo ship carrying capacity of the Allies. Of course, to liven things up in this way was a very difficult task, but any effort in that direction would be of value. The Naval Overseas Transportation Service in this country eventually did splendid work along this line; but there was no such organisation as that in July, 1917. There was no central shipping base and no efficient means of preventing loss of time and cargo space.

One very flagrant case of this was that of the S. S. *Celtic*, which left this country with supplies for Queenstown. No word was sent to Admiral Sims that this ship was bound for Europe until she was almost there, and accordingly no provision for her safe escort into Queenstown had been made; but because of her valuable cargo of food, it was necessary that she have an escort of destroyers, even if those destroyers had already been assigned to the escort of other vessels. When the *Celtic* arrived at Queenstown it was found that she had on board a cold storage cargo, which at that time was not particularly needed and for which adequate storage space had not been provided.

Storage houses were being erected, and if the *Celtic* had arrived two or three weeks later, her cargo could have been unloaded at Queenstown, but as it was, only a small part was removed. The vessel was then ordered to Brest to discharge as much of her cargo there as was wanted, and then returned to Queenstown to await the completion of storehouses. This meant that the ship had to be escorted to Brest and back again, when the destroyers might have been otherwise employed in escorting ships whose cargoes were more urgently needed than that of the *Celtic*.

This is just one of the many cases in which lack of centralization caused trouble, delay, and even unnecessary losses at sea. In this case, if those in charge of the Navy Department had sent word earlier that she was coming, time and effort would have been saved; but better still, if they had gone a little deeper into the matter and made a practice of paying more attention to Admiral Sims' advice and requests, they would have found out that it would be better to send the *Celtic* to Europe with a cargo for which there was a more immediate need. As it was, they sent over a ship whose cargo was not needed and whose unheralded arrival in Europe resulted in the assignment of destroyers to her as a protection, when these destroyers might have been protecting other ships. What was needed was some sort of a central shipping office from which all shipping and cargoes could be routed and from which the authorities in Europe could learn a little in advance what ships and cargoes were to be expected.

The final solution of the matter was a Naval Overseas Transportation Service, the shipping Board, and the British Admiralty, all of which eventually came to an understanding and thereafter worked in unison. Their work aided the convoy system and prevented ships from wandering along the coasts of Europe looking for a harbour in which to discharge their cargoes.

The second manner in which the convoy system could be improved was by increasing the number of anti-submarine craft in European waters. The British were turning out five or six new destroyers monthly; the Navy Department had placed orders for four hundred new destroyers, but of course these would not be finished for many months. Other destroyers, still on this side of the Atlantic, were being sent over every month, and by August about thirty-five of them were operating in Europe. But more were wanted, for half of the ships leaving and entering British ports did so unescorted.

In July, Admiral Sims urgently recommended that every available ship capable of maintaining a speed of fourteen or fifteen knots and of weathering the seas be sent to Europe. He rightly believed that the submarine sinkings would decrease in proportion to the number of anti-submarine vessels employed in Europe.

There were many patrol boats operating along the Eastern American coast, very few of which were necessary and many of which could be of far greater use in European waters. No submarines were operating in American waters, but a great many were operating in European waters. There was little likelihood that submarines would be sent to the American coasts until their mission in Europe had failed, for the time consumed in transit to and from America—a submarine can only make 120 miles a day on a long cruise—could be more profitably spent in English waters.

Also, the sending of submarines to American waters, where shipping was very scattered, would be less productive from the submarines point of view, than keeping them around England, where the shipping was very congested. Admiral Sims maintained that the critical area of the submarine war was the location in which the submarine had to be fought and the area in which it would either fail or succeed. In June and July, it was not failing; in fact, it was still succeeding, because the Allies did not have a sufficient number of anti-submarine craft with which to combat it.

Of course, if the majority of the patrol boats on the Eastern American coast were sent to Europe the coast would be unprotected while America was in a state of war, and to this condition of affairs the American people might have objected. But at that time, as no submarine had been sent to the American coast and as there was not much likelihood of one being sent over for at least several months, the hundreds of patrol vessels on our coasts were really doing no good at all.

This request from Admiral Sims in Europe was met by plans for the construction of more chasers and the conversion of more yachts into war vessels; some of which were being sent over. These all helped out and all played an important role, locally. But Admiral Sims' requests and recommendations not always met with approval in the Navy Department, and many more should have been dispatched than were. The chasers and destroyers were of the most value; the destroyers were ordered to Brest, Queenstown, and Gibraltar, and the chasers to the island of Corfu in the Mediterranean and to Plymouth, England. The destroyers took up their work with their colleagues which had arrived before them, while the chasers became involved in a new form of anti-submarine tactics.

CHAPTER 5

Further Developments

By the Fall of 1917 the critical period of the submarine war was passing. In April it had appeared that the Germans, by sinking a million tons per month, might win the war; in fact, if Germany had continued to sink this amount of tonnage, victory would have been hers; but the sinkings rapidly decreased after the introduction of the Convoy System, which was made possible by the addition of the American destroyers to the existing anti-submarine forces. By November the sinkings amounted to only 30% of their total in April. The situation was in hand, and the submarine campaign had been sufficiently checked to relieve the Naval Authorities of that keen worry which they had experienced in the spring, and called only for a vigorous pursuit of the then existing policies and activities to wipe the submarine off the slate of war as a cause for Allied defeat. Attention now turned toward strengthening the Allied Naval situation as a whole.

In discussing this problem. It must be remembered that though little has been said about the German Fleet, its restriction from the High Seas was of primary importance. Thus, there were two phases to the Naval War; the submarine campaign and the blockade of the German Fleet, which was bottled up at Kiel and other German ports. If the submarine war could be held in check, or the sinkings still further reduced, and the German Fleet kept in its place of hiding, eventual victory for the Allies would be assured.

It had been recognised for some time that though the presence of American dreadnoughts in the North Sea would be of material help to the British Grand Fleet, they would need supplies; and accordingly, the discussion of their coming to Europe had been postponed until the critical phase of the submarine had passed and the shortage of shipping had become less acute. While the submarine war had seemed so critical, it had been felt that the Royal Navy could guard

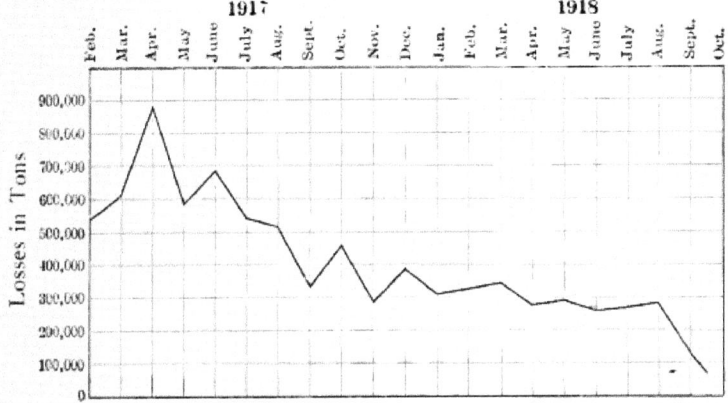

This curve, known as the "Tonnage Curve," shows the progressive success of the convoy system. Its success, during the first few months of its institution, was marked, and thereafter slow but steady. Thus this apparently insignificant curve tells the history of Allied Victory and German defeat, in a very comprehensible manner. It was the author's pleasure to keep this chart up to date each month.

the German High Fleet, as it had done in the past; however, with the dwindling of the seriousness of the U-boat campaign, it was possible to strengthen the British Fleet with American dreadnoughts without making the demands on shipping excessive. In October, 1917, Admiral Sims informed the Navy Department to this effect.

****

He had in July requested the services of four dreadnoughts to be stationed on the western coast of England or Ireland, as protective units against German commerce raiders. The request was not approved by the department.

****

In selecting these dreadnoughts, it was necessary to send over only those which used coal as fuel, for oil burners would have demanded the service of tank steamers, at a time when gasoline was already scarce enough in England and France. Five of the latest and largest American coal-burning vessels, under the command of Rear-Admiral Rodman, U. S. N., were ordered to Europe by the Navy Department in November, 1917, and on December sixth joined the British Grand Fleet as the 6th Battle Squadron under Admiral Beatty in the North Sea.

The British Grand Fleet had been on duty in the North Sea since the outbreak of the war. It had been a fortunate coincidence that in July, 1914, the entire fleet had been assembled for its annual manoeuvres; since that time, it had remained intact in the North Sea. Incidentally, Germany often claimed that this was proof of England's desire for war. Occasionally, scouting vessels of the two nations had encountered each other and short, running fights had ensued; the only combat of any importance had been the Battle of Jutland, which took place on June 1st, 1916.

On that day the British Grand Fleet was at sea in one of those sweeping cruises periodically undertaken for practice, manoeuvring, and general exercise of the various units. In the afternoon, when about 100 miles from Heligoland, a portion of the British Fleet met squadrons of the enemy and an all-night fight ensued. The meeting of the two fleets was proven to be purely accidental, for neither fleet knew that the enemy was abroad. After the battle, in which the losses in capital ships were nearly equally divided, but in which Germany's losses in smaller vessels was far greater than those of the British, both fleets claimed the laurels of the conqueror. Germany, according to her custom, did a good deal more shouting than England after this encounter, for whereas the British authorities had hoped that the en-

The 6th Battle Squadron of the British Grand Fleet made up of five American dreadnoughts here seen on patrol in the North Sea.

gagement would prove decisive in their favour, it did not; they had to content themselves with learning later that the German Fleet had retired to its base, never to attempt another exodus.

Before and after the Battle of Jutland, the duties and policies of the British Grand Fleet had always been one of "watchful waiting." it was very careful watching, but very dull waiting. In the words of an old English tar, who had apparently spent most of his life in the Royal Navy, "Floatin' around that blinkin' Nor' Sea, waitin' till those bloddy 'uns get grit h'enough to fight, and yet always 'oping that they will fight some di, 'tis'nt the kind of life for an h'ambitious or warlike chap the likes of me." Ambition or no ambition, life was pretty dull in that fleet. Day in and day out, flotillas of destroyers and squadrons of cruisers would wander forth, hoping for a chance of action with the enemy. Day in and day out, the tremendous battle cruisers and dreadnoughts would lie at anchor, ready to proceed to sea at two hours' notice.

"Monotonous and boring" describes it best; but "watchful waiting" was necessary. While the British Fleet, whose location was usually about Scapa Flow, stood in readiness to smash a German exodus, England commanded the surface of the sea. Whether she had command of what went on beneath the sea a few months before was another matter, but the command of the surface of the sea, which meant no German ships on the high seas of the world, was of vital importance if the Allies were to win the war.

At last, it seemed that the men of the fleet were to be rewarded. During the first few days in November, 1918, the Admiralty Intelligence Service gained the information that the German High Seas Fleet had been ordered to sea. Excitement in all naval and official circles was rampant. After four years of waiting, "*Der Tag*" had come! Squadrons of destroyers and cruisers were immediately dispatched to meet the enemy. For days these vessels searched, in hopes and in vain, for no enemy ship was seen. Finally, the Armistice was signed, and the victorious units were recalled—victorious without having fired a shell. "*Der Tag*" had come and gone!

Two weeks later the German Fleet surrendered. The entire British Fleet in battle formation went out to meet it and between the lines of the combined American and British Squadrons, the Germans were escorted back to Scapa Flow. A very prominent British naval official, now retired, expressed the opinion that the surrender of the German Fleet without a shot was a disgrace to the naval profession:

In no previous case in history, has a naval command surrendered in cold blood, without even putting up a bluff at a fight. An act of cowardice such as this, degrades the naval profession.

The American Squadron formed only one-eighth of the forty-seven first-line dreadnoughts assembled in the British Grand Fleet. This is a comparatively small proportion, but these five vessels were of great material and moral help to the Royal Navy.

Their arrival in the long dark winter months was a source of cheer to our Allies, the English, and, to a certain extent, a novelty; and anything that was novel was welcomed in Scapa Flow. In looking over the records, one cannot help but be impressed with the commendations received from the British Admiralty for the efficient up-keep of our vessels. During the year that they were in the North Sea they were the source of very little trouble to the British Dockyards.

BANTRY BAY

Admiral Sims stationed another three U. S. dreadnoughts at Berehaven in Bantry Bay, the most Southern point of Ireland. These vessels were ordered to Europe in August, 1918, under Rear-Admiral Rogers, U. S. N., to be used in the pursuit of an enemy raiding vessel should one escape the North Sea patrol. In 1915 and 1916, two enemy raiders had escaped, the *Seeadler* and the *Wolf*, and had done a great deal of damage to shipping. The *Wolf*, during her cruise, in which she covered the greater part of the Atlantic and Pacific Oceans, destroyed over 100,000 tons of shipping, and then managed to get back into Germany. (*Wolf: Raider! Three Accounts of the Imperial German Navy Armed Commerce Raider, SMS Wolf, During the First World War* by A. Donaldson, F. G. Trayes & John Stanley Cameron-Leonaur 2017.)

In the summer of 1918, it was thought probable that with the coming of the long and dark winter months, another attempt to send raiders out would be made. A ship with no lights and a little luck, could sneak past the North Sea patrol during the long hours of darkness, regardless of how efficient that patrol might be. Let the reader try to find another person moving about a pitch-black room, and he will appreciate the impossibility of preventing the egress of a raider in the North Sea.

For this reason, it was good strategy to have fast ships with a powerful armament stationed at a point, such as Berehaven, from which the high seas and broad Atlantic are very accessible. A raider in escaping would naturally, after passing the North of Scotland, turn South, and proceed Eastward between Iceland and the British Isles; Bere-haven, therefore, was the logical situation for these dreadnoughts.

It may be thought that cruisers would have been more serviceable in the pursuit of raiders, and probably in hunting down a merchant ship converted into a raider they would have been; but, in that raiders had escaped before, it was believed not unlikely that in the coming winter enemy battle-cruisers or other heavily armed vessels might undertake to play the role of raiders. The armament of such vessels would be as powerful or more powerful than that of cruisers, and therefore dreadnoughts with their big guns would be of greater ser-vice in hunting them down. Unfortunately, the armistice cut short the possibility of these ships being of use.

CHAPTER 6

The Northern Mine Barrage

It will be recalled that in May, 1917, when the situation had looked so bad, the use of mines on a large scale was not considered wise because such mines did not exist and their construction would have taken too long to warrant their adoption as the primary method of fighting submarines at a time when anti-submarine methods had to be put into effect immediately. In November, 1917, the submarine war had assumed the aspect of a thorn in the side of the Allied Naval position rather than as a cause for defeat. The sinkings were steadily getting less and were soon to be replaced by new construction. However, these losses, and the efforts necessary to prevent greater losses, were becoming more and more expensive to the Allies in manpower and resources.

Much time, many men, and enormous expenditures could be saved, if the submarine was checked still further. But how could this be done? Every available self-propelling ship in England was already employed in fighting it. Similar vessels were being sent over from America in as great numbers as the Navy Department deemed practical. What new tactics would be of further avail? The Naval Authorities came to the conclusion that the end desired could be obtained by bottling up the submarines in the North Sea; this to be accomplished by laying a barrage of mines across from Scotland to Norway.

The history of mine laying in the war up to this time had been interesting. When the submarine campaign began, many a man in drawing-room or bar-room could tell the Naval Authorities that the way to remove the submarine from the ocean was by bottling them up with mines laid in front of their ports of exit. This was good sense, for the proverbial school-boy has always laid tacks in front of the instructor's door when the prank-playing youths wished to hamper his exit. But perhaps many a master, on discovering the tacks, has taken

A floating aerodrome, H.M.S. Furious and her sister ships were commonly known as the "hush ships." Their task was to launch seaplanes to serve as the eyes of the fleet in engagements.

a broom and swept them all aside. Now this was practically the same experience with the Allies in attempting to bottle up the German submarines in their own ports.

An English mine-layer would sneak fairly close to a German submarine base and, under cover of darkness, lay mines along the route of exit. One German submarine might come to grief on these mines, but thereafter all entrances to all submarine bases would be swept by mine-sweepers daily. The same is true about the German submarines laying mines off British ports. The submarines would lay mines during the night off some harbour and the following morning they would all be swept up by British sweepers. Mine fields, to be successful, must be laid in regions where the enemy is not free to sweep them up. Attempts to bottle up submarines in their own harbours proved useless.

New locations for mines were then sought. As we look at the map of Great Britain, we immediately see that the Dover Straits afford excellent natural advantages for the laying of a mine-field. Mines had been laid early in the war to prevent an exodus of German raiders through this short route to the high seas; mines and nets, it was decided, would also be instrumental in keeping submarines out of the English Channel, across which every British Tommy had to travel to get to France. In this operation, nature favoured the Germans, for it was soon discovered that no anchor or cable, however great, could withstand for any length of time the swift current through the Straits. Cables and anchors might hold for a short time, but with the swift tides changing direction every six hours, one or the other, or both, eventually would let go.

In the meantime, submarines continued to use the Dover Straits almost at will. A submarine would get home through the Straits after a cruise, and her Commanding Officer would immediately tell his fellow officers just how he did it, thereby allowing others to pass through in the same way. Finally, under the command of Vice-Admiral Sir Roger Keys, R. N., in the first half of 1918, a movable barrage was laid across the Straits. This barrage, or rather the locations of series of mine fields, could be occasionally changed, thereby eliminating the possibility of German submarine commanders discovering the leaky passages (which will occur in all mine-fields).

Some of these mines were laid in strings and connected by wires; when a submarine was known to be trying to pass through the field, the mines would be exploded from the shore by an electric current. By August, 1918, the Dover Straits were practically closed to German

The American mine laying squadron proceeding to sea on mine laying excursion.

submarines, thereby forcing them to proceed to their respective theatres of operations *via* the North of Scotland.

There were many British mine areas other than those of the Dover Straits. The entrances to practically all the ports of England were very thickly sown with mines, to prevent submarines interfering with departing and entering ships. The Channel in particular was thickly sown. I had the unpleasant experience to be on board the U. S. S. *Piqua*, a yacht based at Brest, when that vessel broke down along the edge of an enormous mine field a few miles East of Plymouth. The heavy wind blew us into the thick of it, and we were immediately informed by the shouts of the men on trawlers that we were in danger, a fact which we already knew too well. Incidentally, I remember trying to determine whereabouts on the ship I would be in least danger should we come to grief. I came to no conclusions, for before I had found such a place, we were safely out on the other side.

Mine-fields of this kind accounted for many submarines during the course of the war. They were, of course, not removable by the Germans, as they were in waters controlled by the British, just as the German mine-fields in the Skagerrak, North of Denmark, were unremovable by the British. The enemy usually discovered the location of the British fields, but this did not help him much, for a submarine commander, once cognizant of a mine-field in the vicinity, was sure to be very careful. Other mine-fields were sown in the North Sea in large quantities, but these, though they did prove effective, did not prevent submarines from passing out into the high sea. And this is what the Naval Authorities finally decided the barrage from Scotland to Norway would accomplish.

All the mines used up to this time had been of the "contact" type, which means that the mine exploded when struck by a ship. On the outside of the mine there were four or five pins about eight inches long; when one of these was struck, as by the side of a ship, it was driven into the interior, the mine exploded. There were other types of "contact" mines, the detonating apparatus of which was of the same principle but differently carried out, in that in the place of pins, a bar on the top of the mine, would cause the explosion. Mines of this type would not be really satisfactory in the proposed scheme, for too many would have to be laid.

There were also those types which could be exploded from the shore by electricity, but these also would not answer the purpose in such a broad area. What was wanted was a mine whose effective radius,

U. S. N. 404. A "Fleet" of mines. Steam winches were used to haul trains or "fleets" of 20 to 40 mines each, aft to the "feeding section." There the mines were seized by gangs of 4 men, who pushed each mine in turn up to the trap at the stern of the ship. Each time the trap opened one mine was released to go overboard. Above the mines is seen a marker buoy, used to mark the end of a mine-field when it was intended to resume that line on a subsequent excursion.

or radius of danger, would be comparatively large.

When America declared war on Germany, many inventions to be used against the submarine began to pour into the Navy Department. Among these was the handiwork of one Mr. Ralph C. Brown, of Winchester, Mass.; his invention was exactly the sort of mine which was wanted for this Northern Mine Barrage. The principle was this: Attached to the mine were four or five very fine wires about 50 yards long; these wires were light enough and had sufficient buoyancy to keep them from sinking and so remained extended beneath the water, stretching with the current or in all directions at the same depth at which the mine was placed.

Any large steel object, such as a ship, coming in contact with these wires, through the agency of an electric battery in the mine, would set an electric current in motion, which would explode the mine. Too much credit can never be given Mr. Brown for this invention, for it made the Northern Mine Barrage possible.

When the idea of laying a barrage of mines from Scotland to Norway was taken up seriously in November, 1917, it was opposed in various circles, for some regarded it not unlike a Jules Verne yarn. It was also argued that it would entail terrific expense and that perhaps the "game would not be worth the candle," or that it would be almost impossible; Admiral Beatty, himself, opposed it on the grounds that it might hamper the operations of the Grand Fleet. But Admiral Sims and those who believed in it, by sticking to their point and showing the possibilities of the scheme and its potential results, won out, and plans for laying the largest field of mines of which man has ever dreamed were begun. In the development of the plans, a discussion arose over the exact location of the barrage.

Practically all agreed that it should be laid between the most Northernpoint of Scotland and the Norwegian Coast, but many were in favour of leaving an open passage of 30 miles near the Scottish Coast. Admiral Sims opposed this strongly, for he argued that there would be no object in spending millions of pounds or dollars in the construction of a mine-field 240 miles long, and then in that mine-field leaving an opening of thirty miles, when it had been found almost impossible to close an opening twenty-one miles long, such as the Dover Straits. He said that if patrol vessels with the help of mines could not shut the Dover Straits to enemy submarines, certainly patrol vessels without the help of mines, could not close this thirty-mile gap. This point became a matter of great discussion, but Admiral Sims forcibly held to his ideas and won. The barrage was made complete, save for an opening a mile wide, near the Scotch coast.

It may be recalled that in February, 1918, Rear-Admiral Earle, Chief of the Bureau of Ordnance in the Navy Department, refused to state before a Congressional Committee the cause for millions of dollars' worth of expenditures, on the grounds that such information was of too secret a nature. Admiral Earle was referring to the expenditures on the construction of the mines for the Northern Mine Barrage. The mines were constructed in this country for the simple reason that, with the extreme shortage of labour in England, America could turn them out much faster. Over 100,000 were made and shipped to Scotland, where they were dumped along the rocky shores of Inverness and Invergordon, two little towns on the Western coast of Scotland, which were to become the United States Naval Mine Force Bases in the North Sea. Eleven old coastwise vessels in this country were converted into the latest types of mine-laying vessels, and sent to Europe; upon their arrival in the North Sea, they were placed under the command of Rear-Admiral Strauss, U. S. N.

Great interest was manifested in all naval circles concerning this barrage. Would it bottle up the submarine, and if it did, would it make the submarine warfare a thing of the past for the remainder of this war? This question was never answered, for the Armistice cut short the mine-laying operations before any definite conclusions could be reached but it was productive of good results, as is shown by the final count of submarines sunk and injured in their endeavours to pass its mesh. Six were destroyed in it, perhaps more, and another seventeen were turned back because injured.

One phase of this great operation, which must not be forgotten, is the size of the task and the heroism of the men who laid the barrage and of those who swept it up. The American and British minelaying vessels used to proceed to sea in these minelaying excursions under cover of one or two squadrons of the Grand Fleet as a protection against enemy assault. The various parts of the mines were assembled at the base and when placed on board the mine-laying vessels were ready for deposit in the sea. The actual laying of a string of 5000 mines only require a few hours. Operations were commenced on June 8, 1918, and thereafter fourteen excursions had taken place, the last occurring on October 25. The total number of mines laid up to November 1st, was a little over 70,000 of which 56,000 or 80% had been laid by our Forces, and the remainder by the British.

As to the heroism of the men who laid this barrage, too much cannot be said. Commander Babcock, U. S. N., Admiral Sims' *aide*, used to say, "Those fellows up there in Scotland are living on the edge of eternity," and the statement was true, for if anything had ever exploded one of these mines, and there were thousands of them scattered along the shore, probably the whole Northern end of Scotland would have been destroyed; the explosion at Halifax in the winter of 1918 would not have been in the same category at all. Or if one mine inside a ship had exploded, and each ship carried seven or eight hundred of them, the vessel would probably have disappeared in fifteen seconds.

However, the human mind becomes accustomed to fear very rapidly and calloused to all thoughts of danger. One officer said that when the task of laying this barrage commenced, an unnecessary cough from any of the navy personnel was almost a court-martial offence, but that after a few months, the striking of a match on the side of one of these mines was an everyday occurrence. No loss of life occurred in this operation through premature explosions; one ship which was carrying mines from America to Scotland, the *Lakemoor*, was destroyed. The degree of success of this barrage will always be open to argument, for it cannot be said that the barrage entirely closed the North Sea as an exit for German submarines to the Atlantic, because in all mine fields, and particularly one of this size, holes and leaky passages will always occur; but it can be said that the moral and material results of the few months' trial gave every promise of success.

★★★★★★★★★★

It proved sufficiently successful in the eyes of the authorities to warrant the construction of a similar barrage between Sicily and the coast of Africa, plans for which were being made at the time of the Armistice.

★★★★★★★★★★

It was a powerful weapon in the hands of the Allies, not as the chief means of defeating the submarine, but as an instrument to that end.

A few of the mines of the Northern Mine Barrage. It can readily be understood that Commander Babcock was right when he said, "Those fellows up there are living on the edge of eternity".

CHAPTER 7

Other Activities

Little has been said so far about the submarine in the Mediterranean, where the U-boat campaign was carried on just as persistently as in the Atlantic and North Sea. The submarine bases in the Mediterranean were at Pola and Cattaro, on the Eastern shores of the Adriatic; both German and Austrian submarines were based here. The German boats were usually brought into the Mediterranean by way of the Atlantic and the Straits of Gibraltar, but in a few cases, submarines had been dismantled at a German North Sea base, and transported by rail through Germany and Austria. The submarines in their operations were favoured by the physiography of the Mediterranean, which, because of its limited size presented many different areas in which traffic was congested.

The Ægean Sea, the waters between the South Coast of Spain and Africa, East of Gibraltar, and between Cap Bon—the Southwestern point of Sicily—and Tunis, are examples of such areas. Trade routes were well established and difficult to alter without lengthening considerably the voyages of the convoys. But though these facts favoured the enemy, the Allies had one great advantage on their side. Every submarine, to gain access to or from the Mediterranean, had to pass through the narrow Straits of Otranto, between the heel of Italy and the island of Corfu. These Straits were very narrow, and presented the same anti-submarine tactical opportunities as the Dover Straits.

The anti-submarine campaign in 1917 in the Mediterranean was being handled by the navies of four nations; England, France, Italy, and Japan. The arrival of the U. S. ships at Gibraltar introduced a fifth combatant. The American vessels worked in unison with the British vessels at Gibraltar, but other than this there was little cooperation. The Allied Naval Council eventually placed the British Admiral at Malta in command of all operations, after much effort and success

Three U. S. submarine chasers in their cove and home at the island of Corfu in the Mediterranean.

had been lost through the lack of unity of command. As soon as co-operation was thus established, earnest attempts were made to close the Otranto Straits to submarines. Heretofore, Naval vessels of France and Italy and Great Britain had been stationed on the Italian coast, working along the barrage of nets and mines. After the establishment of unity of command, all nations were asked to send more ships to the Straits; England immediately sent down one hundred drifters, vessels equipped with listening devices, but not capable of rapid manoeu-vring, and France sent a few destroyers; Italy claimed that her smaller vessels were needed with her fleet. The French and British vessels did excellent work, but the need of high-powered small ships, equipped with listening gear, was keenly felt. (A development of the principle of the old submarine Bell, which at one time was used on all ships; a U-boat running submerged could be heard with these instruments.)

Admiral Sims was one of the first to appreciate this, and so made arrangements to send the first detachment of submarine chasers, to ar-rive from America, to the Straits of Otranto. Thirty-nine of these little vessels under the command of Captain C. P. Nelson, U. S. N., along with their mother ship, arrived at the island of Corfu in the Straits of Otranto, in May, 1918.

The submarine chaser was a very vicious-looking little war vessel for its size. Forward, there was mounted a three-inch gun, and aft, the necessary and elaborate paraphernalia for launching depth charges; a small pilot house stood just forward of amidships, and behind this the mast, at the top of which was a look-out's nest; a wireless was also rigged from the mast. With the help of three high-powered gasoline engines, the chaser had more speed at its disposal than it could often use. It was manned by two officers and twenty-two men.

As the island of Corfu had never been occupied as a Naval base before, the Americans were confronted with the task of converting a barren and uncivilized cove into a modern Naval base. This work was accomplished by the 1,000 officers and men of the crews in a remark-ably short time. Shacks for Staff offices, repair ships, barracks, and a hospital, all had to be erected, but before the end of June the job was completed, and the Forces were ready for operations.

The tactical employment of the submarine chaser was hunting sub-marines in limited areas, with hydrophones and listening devices, and by means of these ascertaining the submarine's course, speed, and posi-tion. When it was definitely located. It was attacked with depth charges according to certain doctrines. The mere method of hunting presented many difficulties. Listening for a submarine, a new development in Naval tactics, required a trained ear on the part of the listener; he had to be able to distinguish the peculiar sound of a "submarine beat" (the noise of the submarine engine and propeller turning over), from that of surface craft, and learn how to ascertain its speed, course, *etc.*

Moreover, one chaser alone could not accurately fix the position of a submarine; to do this it was necessary to have cross-bearings from other chasers. Accordingly, the training of the personnel in their particular duties, was one of the first tasks to be accomplished. It can easily be seen that close cooperation between the various chasers or units was imperative; they had to learn to listen together and to report or communicate the results of their listening to each other and thereby establish the information to govern their attack. While chasers were hunting.

It was also necessary that their listeners should not be hampered by other craft in the vicinity, and hence listening periods of five minutes every hour were established, during which, all vessels in the vicinity stopped their engines to give the chasers a chance to listen for the enemy. In order to prevent the submarine from learning the time set for these periods, during which its engines could be stopped, and between which they could be run, these periods were different every day. As long as the submarine was ignorant of the exact five minutes of the hour designated for listening, it would continue to run, and be the only noise heard, and hence traceable by the chasers. In fact, the personnel of the sub-chasers had a great deal to learn, but they took to their work enthusiastically and soon attained great efficiency.

The first "hunt" at the island of Corfu took place in the latter part of June, 1918, and from then until the Armistice, at least three units, usually four or five (three vessels in a unit) were out hunting day and night. A hunt ordinarily lasted from four to six days, during which time the chances of at least hearing a submarine, or of perhaps getting one, were always good. These chasers carried out more than 32 "hunts" and had some very favourable results. In other words, from the middle of June until hostilities ceased, by means of the smallest war craft in modern use operating 4,000 miles from their home waters, these chasers maintained a constant and tireless watch at the mouth of the Adriatic, by which all enemy submarines sought access to the Mediterranean.

They were rewarded in their work; one submarine was "sunk," while others were probably shaken up or sufficiently damaged to make the submarine commanders abhor the passage in and out of the Adriatic.

The most spectacular operation of the chasers was the attack on Durazzo (on the Eastern coast of the Adriatic) in which British and Italian warships and American chasers took part. The purpose of the attack was to destroy the enemy property at Durazzo and thereby make the place untenable as an Austrian base.

At noon on October 2nd, 1918, the sub-chasers got under way to join the British and Italian Forces, whence they proceeded ensemble to the point of attack. The eleven chasers, under command of Captain C. P. Nelson, U. S. N., were to act as fringes to the main attacking party. On nearing the enemy's coast, all ships came under the fire of the coastal batteries, and several of the big vessels were hit; but the chasers, by means of skilful zigzagging and by keeping first inside, and then beyond the range of the enemy's guns, escaped without casualties.

While this was enough excitement for any of the young crews, none of whom had ever been under fire before, a submarine with its periscope showing, added the choice bit. Chaser No. 215 opened fire at once, and by good shooting forced the submarine to submerge. Chasers *No. 215* and *No. 128* then joined in the attack, dropped their depth charges right above the spot where the U-boat was seen to submerge.

A moment later, subchaser *No. 129* sighted another submarine contemplating malice. This U-boat submerged at once, but then re-appeared a short distance away from sub-chaser *No. 129*, which ran towards it. She dropped two depth charges in a position right over the submarine, but without success, for a few moments later the periscope reappeared and then submerged slowly. Chaser *No. 129* again ran straight for it and when directly over it, let go one depth charge and then two more.

In the meantime, the engagement continued. The encounters with the submarines were over, and there was more work to be done. At the entrance to the harbour, Chaser *No. 130* sighted two floating mines, one of which she destroyed by gunfire; the other she approached just ahead of English destroyers which were following her at thirty knots, causing them to sheer off to the right and pass out of harm's way.

The success of the engagement is well known. All the enemy boats in the harbour were either sunk or crippled, and the base rendered useless for naval or military purposes to the enemy.

Soon after the arrival of the chasers at Corfu, another detachment arrived at Plymouth. Their work was to be the same as that of the Corfu chasers, the actual detail of which has already been described. In this new form of anti-submarine warfare, in which submarines were hunted by means of listening gear, a great deal of experiment and development was necessary. The principle behind it was based on the fact that beneath the water, noises are audible in the form of vibrations; thus, with an electric apparatus, not unlike the principle of the wireless, the noise or vibration of a submarine's propeller against the water can be heard; and by means of another sensitive instrument, a direction finder, which would show the direction whence the noise came, the submarine could be followed, located, and attacked with depth charges.

Admiral Sims in June ordered Captain Leigh, U. S. N., from his headquarters in London to Plymouth to help in the vast experimental work on listening devices which the British were carrying on. There were several different forms of these devices, none of which were perfectly satisfactory, but one of which it was hoped could be developed to a state of reliance. This work was carried on all during the spring and summer of 1918, and though in this time the efficiency and the reliability of listening devices were improved, there was still much to be desired. Captain Leigh's services were of great value in this work. In July two American destroyers, the U. S. S. *Aylwyn* and the U. S. S. *Parker* were ordered to Plymouth and Queenstown, to serve as the flagships of the units when hunting. Commander Cotten, U. S. N., was in charge of the operations.

As to the work of the chasers at Plymouth, a few items of interest show what fine work they really accomplished. In the course of their attacks, they damaged three submarines, one of which was the famous *U-53*, which, it will be remembered, in the summer of 1916 put into Newport; when it proceeded to sea again, it sank several English vessels a few miles off our coast. But the offensive strength of these hunting units was not their only tactical value; they also had protective strength, for the mere presence of vessels equipped with listening gear tended to keep the submarines away. Submarines were also equipped with listening gear, and though they could hear and follow the movements of surface vessels, they preferred not to become too familiar with such units.

Plymouth and its vicinity were favourite areas for submarines, for five submarines per month would usually visit this region. In May, before the chasers began to operate, there were *sixty-five* sightings of, sinkings by, and attacks by, submarines within 100 miles of Plymouth. In July, after they had been operating for two months, there were only *forty-five* sightings of, sinkings by, and attacks by, submarines within the same distance of Plymouth. This shows that the presence of these hunting units in certain areas tended to keep the submarines away. As the months went by, submarine activity in the Channel became less and less.

OTHER ACTIVITIES

It will be remembered that Admiral Sims had given help to the Allied Navies in two ways: first, by fighting the submarine, and then by strengthening the Allied Naval position as a whole. In the execution of the former he had placed American destroyers at Queenstown, Brest, and Gibraltar, and submarine chasers at Corfu and Plymouth; he also was having the American Mine Forces lay 80% of the Northern mine barrage. In the execution of the latter, he despatched dreadnoughts to the British Grand Fleet in the North Sea, and stationed three more at Bantry Bay as a protection against raiders.

There were other ways in which he directed the activities of our forces in Europe to the greatest advantage; he established a base at the Azores and placed submarines at Bantry Bay. In the spring of 1918, he dispatched a cruiser to Murmansk, Russia; during the summer he operated seventy-four cargo carriers which carried coal from Cardiff to France for the army, and finally, he developed a series of Naval Aviation bases in France, England, Ireland, and Italy.

In the Fall of 1917, four submarines and a few yachts and mine sweepers were ordered to the Azore islands under Rear-Admiral Dunn, U. S. N., and a base was established at Ponta del Gada. The Azore islands, situated as they are almost in the centre of the Atlantic Ocean, offered a most desirable locality for an Allied Naval base. Ships, in transit from America to Europe, in need of more fuel or minor repairs could put in to Ponta del Gada and there receive whatever attention was necessary.

The Azores are among the scattered possessions of Portugal, and though Portugal had joined in the war on the side of the Allies, up to the time of our participation, no attempts had been made to establish a base there. It was not probable, but possible, that if the Allies did not have a base at the Azores, the Germans would want one there for

The harbor at Punta del Gado. Two American destroyers, en route to Europe, and an American cruiser are seen in the foreground.

raiders; it was furthermore possible that Germany's large cruiser submarines might attempt to use the islands as a resting place.

To prevent this, Admiral Sims ordered four American submarines of the K-type and some yachts and mine-sweepers to Ponta del Gada. Their duty was chiefly that of patrol, which often became very irksome for only one submarine would visit this region each month and then only for a few days. A great deal of the shipping bound from America to Gibraltar, or *vice-versa*, in passing the Azores occasionally would ask for an escort, which of course was always provided. The chief value of this base, however, was as an aid to Allied shipping rather than as a means of fighting the submarine; many American destroyers, the submarine chasers, yachts, mine-sweepers, and sea-going tugs, which came to Europe, found the facilities extended to the Azores of great value.

In the spring of 1918, Admiral Sims ordered the U. S. S. *Olympia*, an old cruiser and veteran of Spanish War days, to Murmansk, Russia. Murmansk is situated on the Archangel Coast, facing the White Sea. This vessel was to help the various British vessels in that region in their patrol of the White Sea, through which all Allied shipping destined to aid the anti-Bolshevik Forces had to pass. Upon the arrival of the *Olympia*, her commanding officer, Captain McCully U. S. N., in company with the British, took over the control of two or three Russian destroyers, which were lying there idle, and of no use to anybody. Guard duty was the *Olympia's* chief task though on one or two occasions her crew was sent ashore to quiet or prevent local Bolshevik risings.

In the Fall of 1917 seven American submarines were ordered to Europe and stationed at Bantry Bay, Ireland. British submarines had been used against German submarines and their services had been of great value. Admiral Sims saw that a flotilla of American submarines would be of value at Bantry Bay, the Southwestern point of Ireland, past which, German submarines inward or outward bound by way of the North of Scotland to the coast of France, had to pass. In order to prevent Allied ships attacking Allied submarines, systems of recognition signals were established, by means of which, the Allied submarine could immediately make its nationality known.

The destroyers were kept informed of the patrol areas of these submarines, and whenever a submarine was sighted in such an area, the destroyer's officer was careful before he attacked. On one occasion, two American destroyers attacked, and very badly damaged, the British submarine *L-2*, though no loss of life occurred.

The most interesting encounter with the enemy experienced by these American boats, was the case of the U. S. *AL-4* on July 10, 1918. The *AL-4*, under Lt. Commander Forster, was patrolling the waters off Bantry Bay, when a submarine was sighted ahead and a little to the left. The *AL-4* submerged, proceeded towards the enemy submarine, and while thus engaged, heard, by means of listening devices, another German submarine to starboard. Lieutenant Commander Forster turned his periscope towards the origin of the sound of the second submarine, but could see nothing: a moment later a loud explosion took place where the first submarine had been sighted. Nothing more was seen or heard.

For a month or so after this incident, nothing could be learned of the cause of the explosion; later it was discovered that the second German submarine had fired a torpedo at the *AL-4*, and this, missing its mark, had continued on its course, striking the first German submarine and sinking it. This is one of the few occasions in the whole submarine war in which two German submarines were seen together, and on this occasion the presence of these two was accidental, for one was bound south and the other north. It was not their custom to operate in pairs. The task of our submarines was very difficult, particularly so, because of their age; but they stuck to their tasks despite machinery troubles, and forced the German submarines, when passing the Southwestern point of Ireland, to keep a good distance out to sea, away from congested areas.

Another seat of United States Naval operations in Europe was Cardiff, Wales. In January, 1918, Commander J. N. Jeffers, U. S. N., was detached from the U. S. S. *Leviathan*, of which he was Executive Officer, and ordered to Cardiff, a sea coast town in the coal mine region of Wales. His mission was to organise a Naval base from which coal could be transported to France. Many British vessels were based at Cardiff, but as the demands for coal grew, occasioned by the influx of the American Army, more vessels were needed. Admiral Sims answered General Pershing's request for more coal by establishing this base at Cardiff, and cargo ships constructed in America were sent there and employed in what was known as the Army Coal Trade.

The officers and men of these vessels were all of the Naval Reserve Force. In September, 1918, though Commander Jeffers had been made a captain, the duties and work of the base had expanded so greatly that it was necessary to place an admiral in command; Rear-

Admiral Andrews, U. S. N., was selected for this position. At the time of the Armistice, 74 vessels were in service at Cardiff and were employed regularly in carrying coal to Havre, Cherbourg, Brest, and the Western French Ports.

An American Naval Aviation Unit was the first American Aviation Unit to land in Europe. The principal United States Naval Aviation Bases later established were at Killingholme, England; Wexford, Lough Foyle, and Queenstown, Ireland; and Dunkirk and Brest, France. There were also many other stations along the West Coast of France, but these were generally smaller, and many of them were flying schools.

★★★★★★★★★★

Captain H. I. Cone was in command of our Naval Aviation Units in Europe; Lieutenant Commander Atley Edwards was Admiral Sims Aide for Aviation. I have but touched lightly upon Naval Aviation, because I had very little contact with it.

★★★★★★★★★★

The two most interesting bases to study were those of Killingholme and Dunkirk.

Killingholme, on the East coast of England, a few miles from Hull, was the largest of any of our stations. Its work was wholly that of aerial patrol in the North Sea, in seaplanes and blimps. Aerial escort duties formed no small part in helping the handling of convoys within 25 miles of land, for a submarine beneath the water could be seen by an aeroplane long before any destroyers would know of its presence. On one occasion, on August 10, 1918, Ensign Schieffelin, while reconnoitring above the waters to be traversed by a convoy, sighted a dark object beneath the surface of the sea. He signalled to destroyers and then dropped bombs very close to the submarine.

The destroyers came up and, though they could not see it, attacked it and injured it. Eight hours later, this injured submarine, which found manoeuvring extremely difficult, was attacked again by destroyers and sunk. This is one of the many illustrations in which the aeroplane or sea plane has been of infinite value in convoy duty. The value of the aerial escort lay in detecting the submarine's presence rather than as a weapon by which it might be sunk. It is interesting to note that the American Naval Aviators at Killingholme cooperated as one organisation with the British.

At Dunkirk, France, there were located the headquarters of what was known as the Northern Bombing Squadron. This unit was composed of American Naval Aviators who were detailed as a unit of the

Royal Air Force at the Front. Their work was hampered in one way or another by the non-delivery of planes, or such similar incidents, but Captain Hanrahan, U. S. N., who was in command of the unit, realising this fact, lost no time in extending the services of his young aviators to the Royal Air Force. As a part of that greatest Air Force in the war they carried out some excellent bombing expeditions into the enemy's territory. In September, 1918, the Northern Bombing Squadron, upon the receipt of a sufficient number of machines, began to operate as a distinct unit.

By this time the British Army was forcing the German retreat through Flanders and bombing expeditions lost much of their stra-tegical value; but, on the night of October 1, the squadron bombed Zeebrugge and Ostend, as the Germans were evacuating these towns. Unfortunately, the work of the Northern Bombing Squadron, as in the case of the mine barrage and the chasers at Queenstown, Ireland, was cut short by the Armistice before operations were really devel-oped on a large scale. In fact, the Armistice upset a great many plans and spoiled many enterprises.

The Naval Gun Batteries

In December, 1917, the Navy Department informed the British War Office that the Naval Bureau of Ordnance could supply four-teen-inch guns for use in the British Army. The War Office, in that it had guns of a large calibre in use behind the British front, declined the offer and said that they could be used more profitably in some other sector. The department then offered them to General Pershing. He immediately accepted them and asked that they be prepared and shipped to France at the earliest possible moment. These guns were to be mounted on railway trucks, and each gun was to be a self-sustain-ing unit, consisting of eight cars and a locomotive. The guns had been made for the American battle cruisers, but as construction on these vessels had not yet commenced.

It was thought best that these enormous fourteen-inch 50 cali-bre guns be made to serve some purpose in the war. Contracts were placed with the Baldwin Locomotive Works and the Standard Steel Car Company for the construction of the train, and by April, one complete unit was ready for testing. In the meantime the Navy De-partment had issued orders to all large Naval Training Stations to se-lect a certain number of picked men to serve on a mission of special importance and desirability. The selection of these men was one of

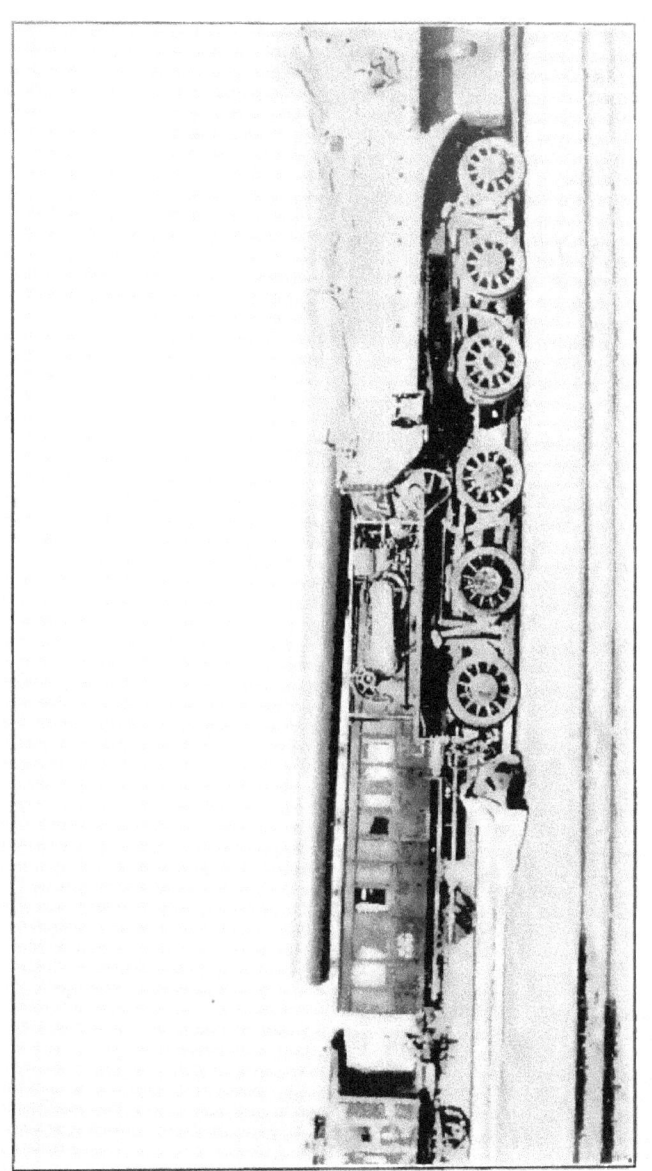

U. S. Naval Railway 14-inch gun at Sommesous.

the most interesting features of the development of the batteries. Each battery train was to have a complement of forty-one men, who. In order to be of the most use, had to be "jacks-of-all-trades."

On May 15, General Pershing was informed that the railway batteries were completed and they were shipped to St. Nazaire; by the middle of August, they were in use at the Front. Their first duty was to fire at the famous German long-range gun, which had been shelling Paris, but the long-range gun moved its position shortly before operations could be begun. Nevertheless, they served at the Front during the remaining months of hostilities and fired a total of 646 rounds. The extreme range of these guns was a little over 42,500 yards, or about twenty-eight miles. The last round was fired on November 11, at 10:59 a. m., one minute before the cessation of hostilities. After the Armistice, Admiral Plunkett, U. S. N., who had commanded the batteries, investigated some of the targets at which the guns had fired and it was discovered that the accuracy attained was equal to any attained during the war.

CHAPTER 8

The Submarines off the American Coast

On May 2, 1918, Admiral Sims sent a cable to the Navy Department with the information that the *U-151* was *en route* to America and might be expected to reach the Coast about May 24. It will be recalled, that in a previous discussion, as to the advisability of sending the majority of patrol boats on the American Coast to Europe in the summer of 1917, it was pointed out that there was no likelihood that submarines would attempt a trip to the American Coast for some time to come. This statement was based on the argument that it was much more profitable for submarines to operate around the British Isles where shipping was congested, than along an extensive coastline, such as that between Newfoundland and Florida.

In the latter part of April, Admiral von Capelle, Chief of the German Admiralty, apparently decided to send submarines to the American Coast. The significance of this new submarine policy will be discussed at the end of the chapter.

On May 15 the *U-151* was in 34° 00' North, and 56° 00' West, (about 900 miles from Cape Cod), and ten days later the news was spread broadcast throughout the United States that a submarine was off the Eastern Coast, and so it was. From then on until September 1st, submarines were operating off our coast. There were four of them in all; the *UK-156* arrived on July 1st, the *U-140* was the third, arriving on July 26, and the *U-117* arrived on August 8.

The *UK-156* first revealed itself not far from Nantucket Light, and on the night of July 3rd off Long Island, laid mines which sank the U. S. S. *San Diego* the following day. It then proceeded North by way of Chatham and Cape Cod to the shores of Nova Scotia; from here it turned South, and then turned North again towards Newfoundland

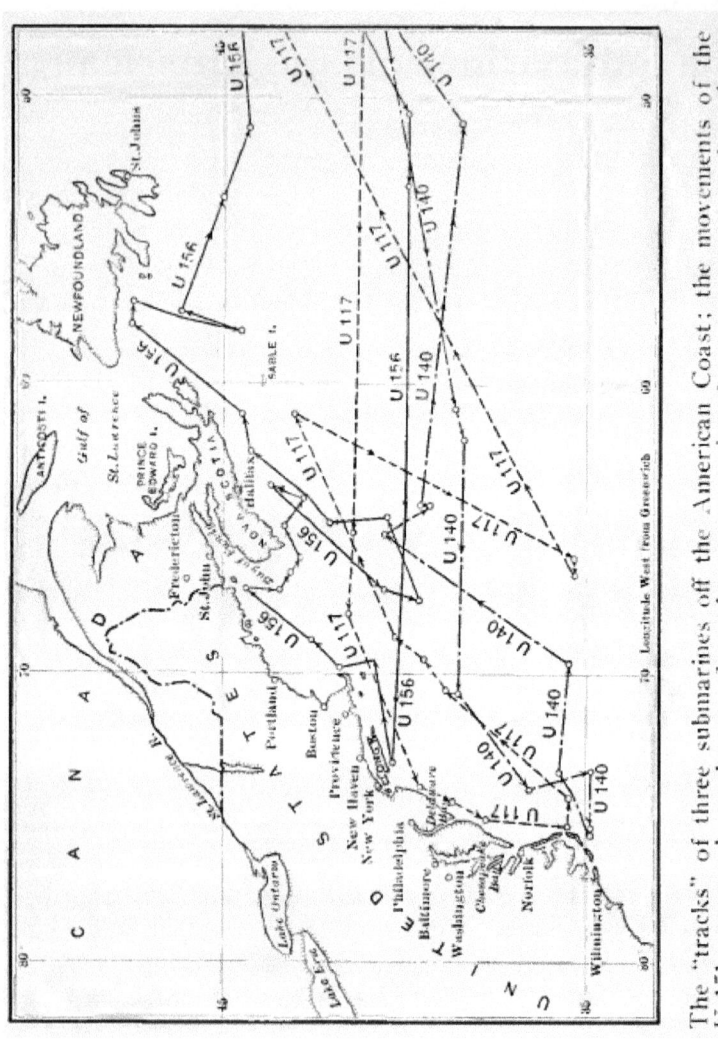

The "tracks" of three submarines off the American Coast; the movements of the U-151 are not here shown. In order to appreciate how vast an area these boats were operating in, and to realize that for that reason their strategical value was small, one must notice that from Norfolk to the edge of the chart is about 1200 miles.

and started for home July 31.

The *UK-140* arrived on July 26, and spent exactly one month in American waters. It cruised up and down the Coast twice, from the Delaware Capes to Chatham, about 300 miles from shore, but was distinctly unfortunate and unsuccessful in its "kills."

The *U-117*, a large mine-layer, arrived on August 8 off Chatham, laid mines off New York, proceeded South to Barnegat, where it laid more, and then continued South to the mouth of Chesapeake Bay and there deposited the rest of its mines. The total complement of mines carried by the *U-I17* was 36, all of which were eventually swept up. On September 2, it was 400 miles out to sea, homeward bound.

During the period that these submarines were off our coast, there was apparently considerable excitement over spies, involving the flashing of lights from the shore, mysterious boats seen at sea, and the danger of a raid from aeroplanes. There is no evidence that any of these submarines wished to have, or ever did have, any communication with the shore, and still less was there ever any chance that aeroplanes could have been launched from the submarines and have raided New York City.

Just how the fear of such an event ever got started I do not know, for why should aeroplanes have been launched from submarines to raid the American Coast, when they had never been launched from submarines to raid the European Coast? it would have been absolutely impossible for these submarines to carry on board an aeroplane, for such an article would have required too much room inside the submarine; and even if a submarine had been made expressly for this purpose, in order to launch it, it would have been necessary to completely assemble it on the high seas.

The success of the cruises of these submarines is undisputed. During July and August, they sank off the American Coast about 20% of the total tonnage sunk in the two months. However, the mere fact that they ventured over here was an admission of failure on the part of the German Naval Authorities, for it meant that they knew that their U-boats could not keep the sinkings up to a high mark by operating in the Eastern Atlantic alone. In other words, it showed that the convoy system in Europe had been successful, for these submarines could have spent the amount of time lost in transit to and from America, five weeks each way, far more profitably in the waters about Great Britain, had not the convoy system protected the shipping so well.

One reason, perhaps, for these submarines coming to America was to satisfy the German people, or more probably give the authorities the chance to inform the German people that German submarines, in their might and prowess, were still winning the war, as could be proved by their operations on the American Coast. Nevertheless, whatever the German Authorities may have claimed, the sending of submarines to America was an admission of failure.

CHAPTER 9

Submarine Operations

There probably has been no more misunderstood phase of the past conflict than that of submarine operations. A submarine campaign, such as Germany carried on, was a new departure in Naval Warfare, and the citizen had nothing but imagination upon which to draw in his version of its execution. I do not by this mean to imply that the submarine war was less cruel than commonly supposed, for that would not be a fair statement. What I do mean, however, is that with no history upon which to base a comprehension of the U-boat war, one's only sources of information were the tales of those who came in contact with it. Stories of those crossing to France, relating how their ship was attacked by seven submarines and missed by four torpedoes, how four of the submarines were sunk and the remainder put to flight, were common.

From such accounts one gathered that hundreds of submarines were at sea at one time, and their deportment not unlike that of porpoises. Now all such tales were grossly exaggerated, and I can say with assurance that very few of our soldiers ever saw a submarine. A short study of submarine operations is interesting, and should dispel all doubt or misconceptions as to the true facts. Let us take for example the situation on August 1, 1918. This of course was more than a year after we had come into the war, but the fundamentals of operation and statistics were practically the same.

On August 1, 1918, Germany had constructed 335 submarines, of which 171 had been sunk; 164 were still operating. (Admiral Von Capelle said that Germany constructed 817 submarines during the war. His statement is not true). There were four different types of submarines, and each was particularly adapted to certain services. Of the 164, (exclusive of the school ships), remaining for service, nine were of the large UK-type, fifty were of the U-type, sixty-five of the UB-type, and 20 of the UC-type; another twenty were used as school ships; twenty of these German boats and twenty-seven Austrian were based in the Adriatic. Deducting the twenty submarines which were in the Mediterranean, Germany had a total of 144 submarines available for service in the Atlantic.

★★★★★★★★★★

The origin of the term U-boat is from the German *Unterseeboot*. Thus, the U-type was the first constructed. The later types were called UB and UC, and UK, the "B" and the "C" and "K" being merely the designation of type.

★★★★★★★★★★

The largest German submarines constructed were those of the UK-type, and these in size were surpassed only by the British K-class, which were driven by steam. All German submarines were driven by Diesel engines on the surface, and by electric batteries and motors when submerged. These UK-boats were 360 feet in length, 36 feet from keel to conning tower, and had a displacement of four thousand tons when submerged. A fairly good idea of their size can be gained by comparing them with a cargo ship, the average displacement of which is about five thousand tons.

The armament consisted of twenty torpedoes, thirty-six mines, eight torpedo tubes, and a six-inch gun fore and aft. On the surface they could make speed of fourteen knots and when submerged only seven or eight. Their complement of personnel was twelve officers and eighty-eight men. This type was designed and used for long cruises in the Atlantic (two of them visited the American coast); they could stay at sea, if a slow speed was maintained, for three or four months.

The U-class was similar to but smaller than the UK-class; boats of this class varied in size according to date of construction. The early U-types were only of 800 tons displacement, the later were of 1,200 tons. The speed of both was about eleven knots on the surface and six knots submerged. The smaller boats carried only eight torpedoes, the larger twelve, the armament of both was a three or four-inch gun fore and aft. The complement of these vessels was thirty-two or thirty-seven officers and men. Both types had a cruising radius of about six thousand miles, and were usually employed in the waters West of England and of France. The *U-58*, which was sunk by the U. S. S. *Fanning* and *Nicholson*, was one of the smaller types of the U-class.

The UB-boats were smaller than the U-boats, and had a displacement varying from 500 to 750 tons. They were armed with a thirty-two-pounder forward of the conning tower, and carried four to ten torpedoes. Their cruising radius varied between four thousand and six thousand miles; they were usually employed in the waters about Great Britain, and were not designed or constructed for deep-sea duty. The third type, the UC-boats, were mine-layers, and of less displacement than the UB-type. They were armed with a twenty-two-pounder forward of the conning tower, and carried eighteen mines, which they would usually lay in the entrance of some harbour and then return to their base.

The average number of submarines in the waters about Great Britain and France, per day during 1917 and 1918, was about twenty-one or twenty-two, though this average sometimes reached as high as twenty-eight and other times as low as sixteen. It would seem that twenty-two submarines, operating with a total of 144 in commission, was a very low percentage but as a matter of fact it was not. The wear and strain on the submarine's machinery and personnel was so great that it was usually necessary to keep a submarine in port for repairs, overhauling, and rest, two or three times as long as the average cruise.

★★★★★★★★★★

In September, 1917, Germany made a great effort to send twice as many boats to sea as usual. The result was that half of them returned in a few days, because they were not really in good condition.

★★★★★★★★★★

It speaks well for the machinery and efficiency of the submarine flotilla that the operating number remained as high and as steady as it did. The average twenty-two boats thus operating would be located generally as follows. There were usually three operating in the North Sea, preying upon the English and Scandinavian traffic; one of them would be a mine-layer *en route* to, or returning from, a mine-laying cruise to the mouth of the Thames or to the Firth of Forth or to a similar point; the other two would probably be UB-boats. Two more submarines, one probably bound for its base, the other for a cruise, would be in the North Sea; both of these would probably be U-boats. North of Scotland and Ireland another two, perhaps both U-boats or one a UK-boat, would be bound in or out.

There was usually one of the UB-type in the Irish Sea and the Bristol Channel. Southwest of the English Channel, where all lanes of shipping converge, there were always at least three U-boats and perhaps more. On July 8, 1918, there were as many as six in this area. Southwest of Brest and along the coast of France a U-boat and a UC-boat might be operating, the latter laying mines outside the harbours of the West coast of France. Off the coast of Spain, or further West, a UK was usually outward or inward bound from the middle Atlantic or the waters about the Azores. The accompanying chart gives a graphic location of the daily positions of submarines as might have been seen on a large map at Admiral Sims' headquarters in London.

I know that the reader is now wondering how submarine positions were known, how their movements were followed from day to day, and how the different types of submarines were recognised as being in this or that area. The answer is, by the splendid work of the British Admiralty Intelligence Service, under Rear-Admiral Sir Reginald Hall. This department of the Admiralty had three sources of information about submarines. First, by radio direction finders, the meaning of which will be explained in a moment; secondly, by an elaborate system of agents in Germany and neutral countries, and thirdly by the cross-examination of the survivors of submarines sunk.

The presence and exact position of the majority of submarines at sea was learned every night by an elaborate system of radio stations along the coast. It was the custom of submarines to communicate with their headquarters in Germany almost nightly by wireless. The messages were always in a highly secret code, and might, or might not, be eventually deciphered by the Admiralty. The chief interest in them was the opportunity they afforded to locate the submarine which sent the message. Every time a submarine wirelessed to Germany, English radio stations would pick up the message.

The wireless instruments at the stations were equipped with an apparatus known as a radio-direction-finder by which the direction or bearing of the origin of the message could be determined to a fraction of a degree. Each station, upon receipt of such a message, would immediately telegraph to the Admiralty in London the exact bearing of its origin from that station. In order to illustrate how the submarine's position was then determined, let us take an imaginary example.

Wireless stations at Land's End, Milford Haven, and Queenstown, have all sent telegrams to the Admiralty stating that a submarine at eleven o'clock at night communicated with Berlin, and that this submarine was in a position bearing due West from Land's End, Southwest from Milford Haven, and due South from Queenstown; these bearings naturally would be given in degrees rather than in terms of West and Southwest. When this information was received by the Admiralty, the officers there on duty would draw lines West from Land's

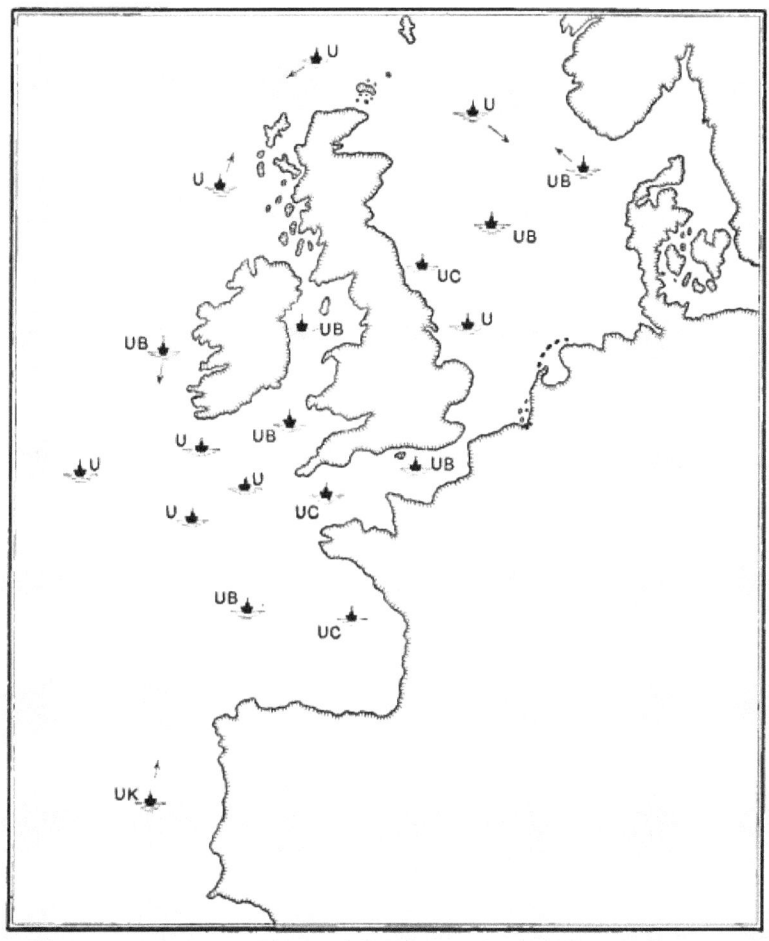

A graphic illustration of the positions of enemy submarines as represented on the daily charts. A pin with a flag attached was used to represent the submarine's location, and each morning each pin was moved according to the submarine's movements of the night before. From this map, the reader will understand why Admiral Sims informed the Navy Department that the place to fight the submarine was in Europe, and that anti-submarine vessels in American waters were of no strategical value.

End, Southwest from Milford Haven, and due South from Queens-town, and where those lines crossed, there would be the submarine.

In this way, practically every submarine could be followed from day to day; I say practically every submarine, because sometimes they did not communicate with Germany at night. Of course, there were other reports of submarine movements, from the sightings of submarines at sea, but many of these were false. The striking or sinking of a ship by a torpedo was a positive proof of a submarine's presence in a certain po-sition; a report of a ship being missed by a torpedo, or the sighting of a periscope, was not. Almost without fail, the positions of submarines, as established by the radio-direction-finder, were the same as the proofs of their positions established by the sinking of a ship.

I remember one very interesting occasion to show the reliabil-ity of the direction finder; it occurred on the night of October 17, 1918. When I arrived at the office the following morning, I found a telegram on my desk stating that the U. S. S. *Kimberly*, a destroyer at Queenstown, during the previous night had located a submarine off Bantry Bay, had hunted it down by means of listening devices, and finally attacked it with depth charges at eight minutes of twelve. In the telegram, the exact position of the attack was given. Later that morning I learned from the Admiralty that the submarine attacked by the *Kimberley* had communicated with Germany by wireless at three minutes of twelve, or five minutes after the attack. The position of the attack—which was of course the position of the submarine at eight minutes of twelve—was exactly the same as the position of the submarine, as established by the radio direction finder at three minutes of twelve.

As soon as the position of each submarine had been worked out on the charts, such information was sent to the different bases or wirelessed to those ships to which the information might be of use. The Admiralty took the greatest care that this method of locating submarines should not be discovered by the enemy, for the authorities regarded it as the greatest secret in their possession; and there is no evidence to show that the Germans ever did discover it.

The second manner in which the Admiralty kept itself informed was by a very efficient system of agents in Germany and neutral coun-tries. The organisation of this system commenced after the Declara-tion of war in 1914 (and the agents themselves were sent to Germany and neutral countries), for previous to 1914 the British Secret Service was of little importance. These agents, some of whom were English women, apparently found many sources of information, not the least of which were deserters from the German Army or Navy. As time went on Germany apparently discovered this and employed men to play the role of deserters, not only in order to catch the British agents, but also to give these agents all sorts of misinformation.

Some of their reports were very heterogeneous and erratic and often the opposite to the true facts; on the other hand, a vast amount of them were good sound truths, which proved to be of inestimable value. The greater part of them dealt with data on the new construction of submarines, assignment of commands (a very important factor in calculating the submarines' probable movements) and much technical information concerning submarine machinery and the construction of torpedoes. The aid which these agents rendered the Allied Cause can never be too highly recognised; the submarine campaign was the vital issue in this war and these men and women, at the risk of their lives as spies, rendered a great and patriotic service in helping to defeat it.

The third method of gaining information about the submarine was by questioning and cross-examining the survivors of submarines destroyed. Previous to 1917, in this country, we all heard that the English Navy refused to take German submarine officers and men prisoners when their boats were sunk. No more fabulous story was ever circulated. The British made all survivors prisoners, and they spared no effort rescuing them; their services as informants of the activities of the submarine flotillas were valuable; to have let them drown would have been a military error. When survivors of a sinking submarine had been rescued, they were immediately taken to a detention camp, and from there, after three or four days of good food and rest, and enough whiskey to make them see the right side of life, brought up to London to be interrogated.

Some of these men were very affable and in return for the kind treatment they had received, gave the interrogators much valuable information; others, through patriotism or hate, would disguise their statements very cleverly, misstating facts just enough to make the sifting out of the truth very difficult. And then there were others who would relate the most dreadful yarns imaginable; but such stories were always recognised as false. The information sought in these seances dealt with the value of various forms of offence and defence in the anti-submarine war, such as the value of depth charges, mines, and nets; and with conditions in Germany in general. As several survivors

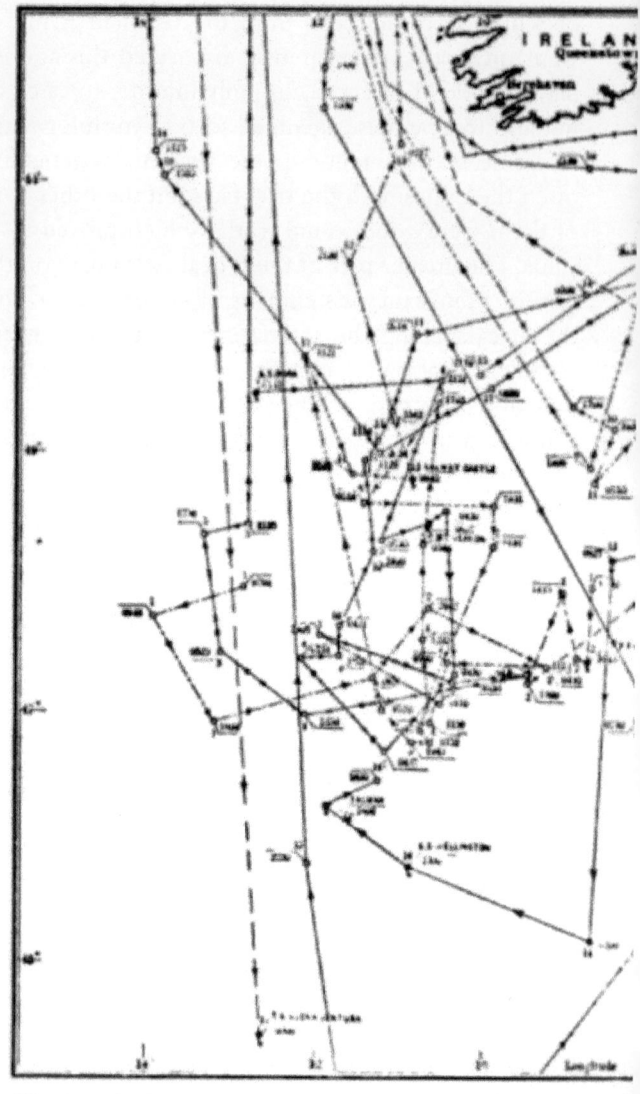

The "tracks" or movements of submarines during the fir
to date daily, and as each new position of each submarin
Each position is shown by a small circle, the date, and hou
time. The majority of the positions were established by m
chart by the hour and date, but without vessel's name. S
were rather famous: notably, those of the "Mt. Vernon,"
zance, the U. S. S. "Chester" narrowly missed running int
In the Irish Sea may be seen the location in which five Q
gow out of convoy. From this chart my statements that t
more about submarine operations than was generally sur

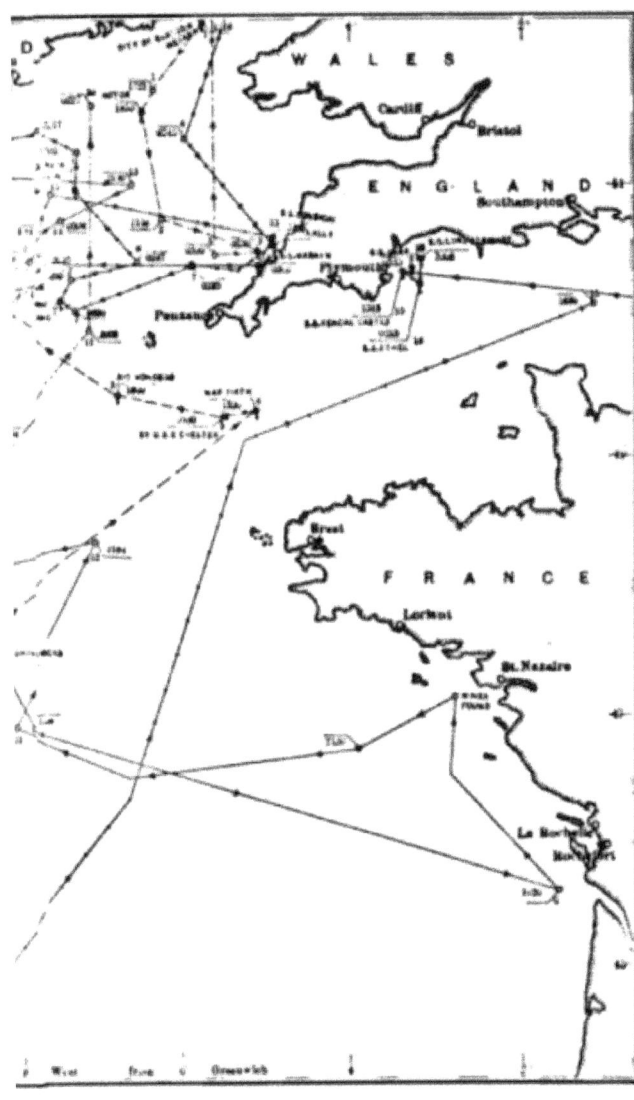

st two weeks of September, 1918. This chart was kept up
ie was definitely established, it was plotted on the chart.
ir, according to the twenty-four hour method of reckoning
iears of the radio direction finder; these are shown on the
iome of the losses, represented by the vessels' names.
' "Wellington," "Kendel Castle,"' etc. Just south of Pen-
o the U-53 on the night of September 5th, in a thick fog.
iueenstown destroyers lost the "Mesaba" and City of Glas-
he British Admiralty and Admiral Sims' staff knew far
msed, are proved.

were taken prisoners each month, and information came in regularly from the agents in neutral countries and Germany itself, the task of learning the trend of events within the borders of the enemy was rendered possible.

It will be seen from what has now been said that the Admiralty Intelligence Service was in a position to keep itself informed at all times. We heard a great deal in England and America as to the efficiency of the German spy system; there were undoubtedly a great many German agents at large in this country, and in Europe. The German spy system was well organised, but it was inferior to the British Admiralty Intelligence Service. Even though the German system was organised many years previous to the war and gained strength by probing into the secrets of, and plotting against, the unsuspecting and trusting nature of the world at peace.

In comparing the information which the Germans had about the Allies, with the information the Admiralty had about Germany, it is easily seen that the calm and practical British mind was far better adapted to picking up true facts, than the bombastic German mind which too often allowed the wish to act as father to the thought. This was proven many times during the war, and the following is an excellent example of the errors made. On July 19, 1918, the H. M. S. *Justicia* was torpedoed and sunk North of Ireland by a German submarine. The *Justicia* was a vessel of 33,000 tons and very similar to the U. S. S. *Leviathan*, formerly the *Vaterland*, in that both vessels were among the largest afloat, and each had three funnels.

The German Admiralty sincerely believed that the *Leviathan* had been sunk. Now if the German Admiralty Intelligence had been on to its job, it would have known that the *Leviathan*, since April, had been running only to Brest and accordingly could not have been anywhere near the Northern coast of Ireland. It may be argued that to learn to what port the *Leviathan* was sailing would be expecting a great deal of any Intelligence Service, but for such purposes an Intelligence Service exists. In this case the Germans had the wrong information, and wrong information is of less use to a military organisation than no information at all.

The British Admiralty Intelligence, on the other hand, to my recollection anyway, never had the wrong and always had the right information. There are many other cases in which the German Intelligence Service showed itself inferior to that of the British, a fact which gave the Royal Navy a tremendous advantage in the submarine war. It is

The highest development of submarine construction. Above, a submarine of the German U. K. type. Below, one of the British K. class, which are steam driven. The latter was larger, faster, and in every form of service, except that of piracy, a better type than the former.

only proper to mention here the courtesy and trust shown by the Admiralty in allowing Admiral Sims and his staff the use of secret information.

But to return to the discussion of the operations of submarines. I said that the average number operating on any given day would be about twenty-two, not including those in the Mediterranean where the average would be about six or seven. The average length of a cruise, excluding the cruises of UK-boats, which would be about three months, was about three or four weeks. This means that one submarine left its base in Germany and one returned about every day. The bases of the submarines were at Kiel, Bremerhaven, Wilhelmshaven, Brundesbuttel, and in Flanders, at Zeebrugge, and Ostend. From these bases they would set out, pass through the Dover Straits, or more likely, particularly in 1918 after the Dover Straits had practically been closed by mines, pass North by way of Scotland, and out into waters West of the British Isles.

No submarine officer when he set out ever knew how long his cruise would be; he would have on board food and fuel enough for five or six weeks, but the chances were that he would not have to stay out that long. The factor which determined the length of the cruise, was the rapidity with which the torpedoes were used. The number of torpedoes carried, of course, was varied and limited, some of the smaller boats carrying only eight and the larger ones sixteen or twenty. Thus, a submarine would stay at sea until all of its torpedoes had been spent in sinking or injuring vessels; this would usually take two or three weeks, and the remaining week or so of the average cruise would be consumed in passage to and from the various theatres of operations.

The cruises of mine-layer submarines were usually shorter than those of the other types, for these boats would proceed to the point where the mines were to be laid, lay them and return to the base immediately. Submarine commanders usually received but few instructions from their flotilla commander at the base; the individual officer aboard the submarine was a better judge of his own abilities under various conditions than the admiral at the base. The only orders usually given dealt with the areas of operations, and the vicinity in which the submarine was to operate; and this was only done to the extent of insuring against the super-concentration in one area and the total absence of submarines in another.

Intelligence information showed that the same commanding officers, regardless of the submarine they commanded, usually visited the same area on each cruise. This was natural enough, for without the use of many of the former coastal lights, navigation at night was extremely difficult, and the better acquainted an officer became with a certain region the more efficient his operations were. This was particularly true of the officers of the mine-layers. An officer had to know his ground well to lay mines effectively in the entrance to harbours; he was allowed to deposit them where he saw fit, and naturally he would choose a locality with which he was familiar.

Quite contrary to the general impression of the submarine campaign, there is absolutely no evidence to show that U-boats ever had any bases except in the enemy countries. There was much fear expressed in many quarters, upon our entry into the war, that submarines would establish bases in Mexico, or in the West indies; but they never did. The only place which might have been used as a base, if there was any advantage in having one, would have been the Azores, and Admiral Sims established a base there himself. The Azores, however, would probably have been used as a base for raiders, rather than for submarines.

After all, what would have been the benefits to be derived from having a base for submarines anywhere except where the services of a Navy Yard were available? I have shown that the length of a submarine's cruise was dependent upon the rapidity with which the torpedoes were consumed, for more supplies and fuel were carried than usually were required. If a submarine wanted food, it would merely have to stop a few sailing vessels and help itself. The only use then of a base would be as a place in which repairs could be effected and torpedoes provided, and I question whether either repairs or torpedoes could be made along the Western Coast of Ireland, or at the Azores, or in the West indies, or Mexico.

It is true that occasionally a submarine would put into a Spanish port for minor repairs or a brief rest, but if the Spanish authorities allowed it to stay more than twenty-four hours without interning it, as provided in international law, the British, American, and French Consuls soon saw to it that the submarine was either ordered out of the port, or interned. It is also known that in one case a submarine stopped at an island on the Northwest Coast of Ireland and that there the crew went ashore and shot some wild sheep for fresh meat. But outside of this there are no cases, with proofs to back them, in which submarines ever even tried to make use of any locality as a base. The

The German submarine base at Bruges. The submarines were kept inside the shelters when in port to protect them from air-raids. Note the size of the shelters compared with the man standing on the left.

German submarine bases and Navy yards had a sufficiently difficult task to keep the submarines in good condition, without trusting to the facilities provided by a barren island or cove, or in the naval genius of Mexico.

Whenever we used to hear of an attack on a ship or transport, there were always at least two submarines present and sometimes four or five or more. These tales were invariably exaggerated and false, for it was not the policy of the submarines to operate together. In the first place, one torpedo was sufficient to sink almost any vessel; if a second submarine stood by and watched the other submarine fire the torpedo and do the sinking, its presence was useless. If it took part in the attack and fired a torpedo, its efforts were wasted, for one submarine would be very nearly as sure of getting its prey as two of them together. The story of the U. S. S. *AL-4* on July 10, 1918, will be recalled. In which two submarines accidentally became mutually interested in the *AL-4* and before they had finished, the one had sunk the other. There are other cases on record in which the presence of two submarines was only a hindrance or serious menace to both of them.

Attacks on ships were of two kinds: those in which the submarine would stop a sailing vessel or steamship by gunfire, and sink her by placing bombs in the hold, and those in which the submarine would fire a torpedo at the vessel, submerge, and try to effect an escape. The former sort became less numerous as more ships were armed, and after a few submarines had encountered British mystery ships, the torpedo attack became prevalent. Imagine a steamship on the horizon. The commanding officer of the waiting submarine would approach nearer to the vessel to ascertain her course and speed, which, of course, he must know in order to be able to fire a torpedo accurately.

Dazzle painting or camouflage was used on ships to make them less visible. This application of protective coloration was good in theory, but on the open sea with the vessel's mast and hull standing out above the horizon, streaky painting of lights and shadows had little effect. There were cases, I suppose, in which, because of camouflage, a submarine officer found it difficult to make out the exact types of ship he was to attack. For instance I remember when I was attached to the U. S. S. *Leviathan*, in March, 1918, that one of the destroyers, escorting us into Liverpool, appeared to have only two funnels, (all American destroyers have either three or four funnels), and that several of us remarked upon it at the time.

A few moments later, the sun came out from behind a cloud and

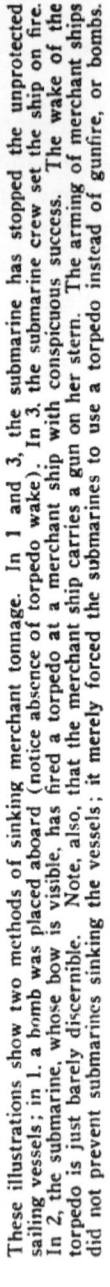

These illustrations show two methods of sinking merchant tonnage. In 1 and 3, the submarine has stopped the unprotected sailing vessels; in 1, a bomb was placed aboard (notice absence of torpedo wake). In 3, the submarine crew set the ship on fire. In 2, the submarine, whose bow is visible, has fired a torpedo at a merchant ship with conspicuous success. The wake of the torpedo is just barely discernible. Note, also, that the merchant ship carries a gun on her stern. The arming of merchant ships did not prevent submarines sinking the vessels; it merely forced the submarines to use a torpedo instead of gunfire, or bombs.

we saw the third stack. This destroyer was camouflaged, and under certain conditions of light we had been deceived in her appearance. The submarine commander, however, did not care to definitely make out the sort of ship his prey was; what he wanted to know was what course he should steer in order to intercept her, or in other words, in what direction was the ship going. In order to determine this, he would look at the masts and funnel. (If the ship were running parallel to him, he could determine this immediately.) The closer together the two masts and funnel were in his periscope picture, the nearer directly towards him the ship would be coming.

If the mast on the left was higher than the one on the right, he would know that the left mast was the forward mast and hence the ship was approaching him on a course to his left; and if the right mast was the higher mast, he would know that the ship was approaching to his right. If the masts and funnels had a "rake" to them, that is if they slanted a trifle aft, his estimate of the course of the ship would be made much easier. For this reason, camouflage, according to experience and statistics, did not prove of value in preventing his gaining this information. It only continued to be applied throughout the war because merchant crews gathered a certain sense of confidence from having their ships painted in this way.

What did help out though, was the erection of straight masts and funnels, all as short as possible, with the after mast a little higher than the forward one. This arrangement gave no information one way or the other to the submarine officer as to the ship's direction, for with the masts short and stubby, and practically no funnel at all, his chief source of information was gone. With the introduction of the convoy system, camouflage of any sort became entirely useless.

But to return to the attacking submarine. When the submarine had ascertained the speed and course of the merchant ship. It would submerge, periscope and all, and by dead reckoning—which means steering by compass—proceed to a point very near from which it had been estimated a torpedo could be fired. Submarines had to be within one thousand yards or less of a ship to be sure of the torpedo striking its mark. The captain of the submarine would then bring his boat within ten or fifteen feet of the surface, and stick his periscope up to see how matters stood. If all were well, that is if he were within a thousand yards of his prey, a torpedo would be fired and if it hit its mark, he would look around hurriedly to see if any patrol boats might attack him, and then submerge to a depth varying from 30 to 200 feet, and try to make good an escape.

After this attack, some of the survivors would relate that no submarine was seen at any time, while others would tell how the ship was attacked by three submarines, two of which were rammed and sunk. The former tale would, of course, be the correct one, but the latter tale would be the one more popularly told, and in this way much misinformation was spread. There were many cases where ships were sunk and the submarine never seen, even though destroyers were present. The most ideal conditions under which a submarine could attack a ship, was from a position between the ship and the sun.

When a submarine attacked a convoy under the escort of destroyers, the submarine officer's task was more difficult. A convoy was always zigzagging, which meant that the submarine, if it came too close to the convoy, would always run the chance of being rammed. To avoid getting too close it was necessary to keep the periscope above the water, and this might be seen by one of the watchful destroyers. Often it was believed that a submarine, because of the difficulties involved in an attack upon a convoy, would fire a torpedo at the middle of the convoy and trust to good fortune that it would hit something. As soon as a ship in convoy had been torpedoed, the excitement for the submarine began.

A torpedo leaves a wake behind it, and though the destroyers did not see the submarine or its periscope, its general vicinity could always be found by following the wake to its origin, where depth charges would be dropped; and though these might not sink it, the submarine and its crew could expect no good from such under-water explosions.

During the hours of daylight, and at night, submarines used to run alternately on their Diesel engines and storage batteries: on the surface the engines were used, and when submerged, the batteries and motors. By running on their engines for a few hours, the batteries were charged; they were kept almost fully charged, in order to have enough current to allow for a long-submerged run, should anti-submarine vessels be on the trail of the submarine. The crews of course preferred running on the surface for at such times they were allowed to go up on the conning tower and smoke and enjoy the air. Sometimes, when attacked by anti-submarine vessels, or in storms when operations were impossible, if the bottom was sandy and the water shallow, submarines would rest there for several hours.

However, as the waters in which they could rest on the bottom were necessarily shallow, a seaplane overhead could distinguish the shadow of the boat beneath the waves, and call anti-submarine craft to attack it. Resting on the bottom was not generally a safe practice. The safest method of procedure for a submarine was to stay on the surface as much as possible, and maintain a good watch; in this way ships could be more easily sighted, and by submerging, approaching destroyers could be avoided.

A good idea of the life on the submarine is gained by the following extracts from the report of Lieutenant Isaacs, U. S. N., who was taken prisoner on the *U-90* when the *President Lincoln* was sunk on May 30th, 1918:

> The *U-90* was built in 1916; it is about 160 ft. long, and carries two six-inch guns, one forward and one aft of the conning tower. The captain of the *U-90*, Captain Remy, boasted that he could make sixteen knots speed on the surface and that he had demonstrated the superiority of the speed of German submarines, as compared with the speed of American submarines, sometime previously when he had a 'run-in' with the U. S. Submarine *AL-4*. (At Berehaven.) He said that both submarines had manoeuvred to fire a torpedo at each other and that in so doing both had submerged two or three times and that finally he was able to fire the torpedo at the American submarine after getting into position, which he was able to do because of his superior speed.
>
> Just as he fired the *AL-4* dove and his torpedo passed a few feet over her. Captain Remy never submerged to a depth greater than 200 ft., though he claimed to be able to submerge 300 ft. The last day out, on the way back to Kiel while passing through the Kattegat, he travelled submerged for over ten hours at a depth of 200 ft. I doubt if he could make more than eight knots when submerged. He carried a crew of forty-two men and officers. One officer, Kapitan-Leutnant Kahn was aboard for the purposes of instruction, having had his request granted by the German Admiralty to command a submarine of his own. While I was at Wilhelmshaven Kapitan-Leutnant Kahn came to see me in prison and told me that he had just received orders to take command of a new submarine.
>
> Of the crew of forty-two men, two were warrant officers, one a navigator and the other the machinist. The captain's three assistants were lieutenants, corresponding to our grade of ensign.

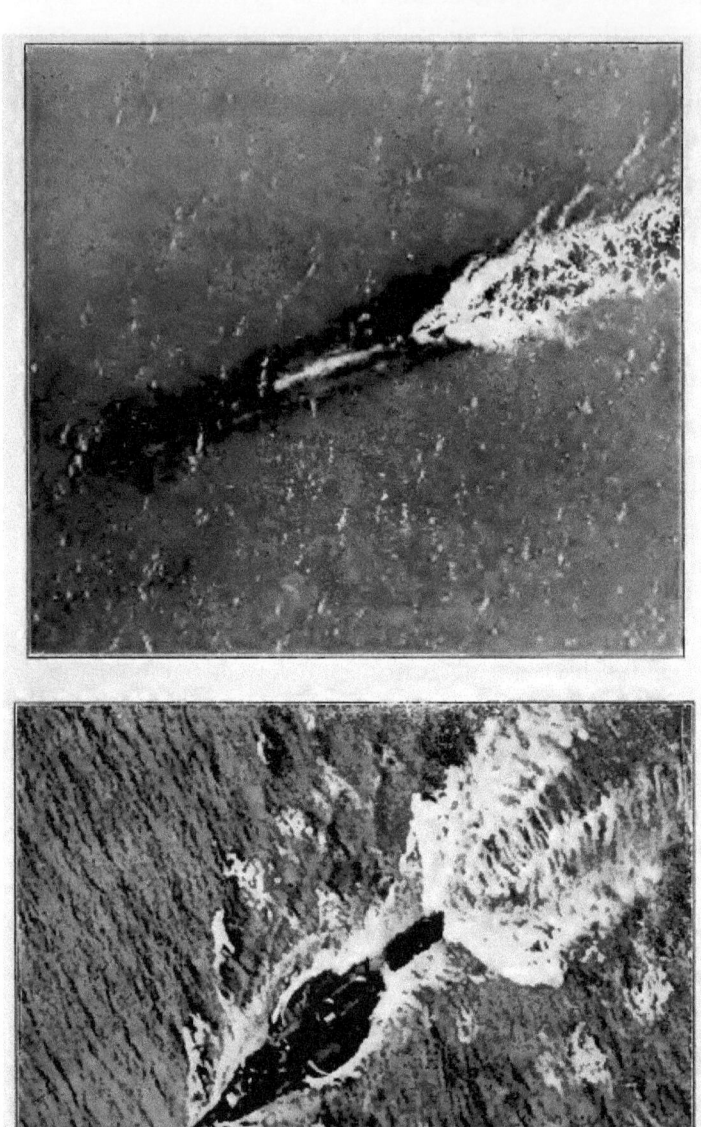

A submarine as seen from an aeroplane. The white foam of the submerged boat is caused by the conning tower which is not altogether under water.

One was a German Naval Academy man, who entered the navy in 1913; he was a deck officer. Another was a reserve ensign from the Merchant Fleet, who spoke English very well, having been in America and England in peace time on various steamers. The other officer was a regular, who had gone to a special school for engineers and he was responsible for the efficiency of the machinery; he did not stand a deck watch. The deck watch was stood by the navigator and the two ensigns.

Captain Remy took the wheel when ships were sighted and when passing through dangerous waters. He had entered the navy in 1905 and had travelled considerably, having been in America in 1911 on a German cruiser which had put in at Charleston, S. C, and into New York, at both of which places he had been hospitably entertained. He liked America but could not understand why America had entered the war. He believed, as all Germans are taught to believe by Governmental propaganda, that our entry into the war must have had as its motive the rendering safe of the millions we loaned to France and England early in the war.

The *U-90* carried eight torpedoes. On this cruise she had sunk only two ships of about 2,000 tons apiece. Captain Remy said that they seldom fired torpedoes at a range greater than 1,000 yards and if possible, he approached to within 500 yards of his prey.

The submarine rolled a little in the Atlantic, though we had no very rough weather. In the North Sea the choppy seas seemed hardly to affect it and under the surface there was no sensation of being in motion. The air inside the submarine when we were submerged on the last day out for ten hours became very disagreeable. However, several tanks of oxygen were carried which could have been used in case of necessity.

The water-tight doors between the different compartments were kept closed at all times after entering the North Sea. The officers and crew smoked in the coming tower or on deck, but nowhere else. The wardroom was about six feet wide and seven feet long and here we ate at a table; the food was kept in lockers in the wardroom.

Here also they put in hammock hooks and swung a hammock for me to sleep in, alongside two bunks used by Kahn and one of the other officers. Just forward of this room was a smaller compartment, known as the captain's cabin, in which he had his desk and bunk, with scarcely room for either. Forward of this cabin was a sleeping compartment for the men and forward of this was the forward torpedo room; I was never allowed to enter the torpedo rooms. Aft of the wardroom on the starboard side was a small cabin, about four feet wide and six feet long, occupied by the other two officers. Across a passage on the port side was the radio room and aft of this was the control room; here there were always two men on watch.

Aft of the control room was the other living compartment for the men, and here the food was cooked and meals served. Aft of this was the engine room and the after-torpedo room. The men slept in hammocks and on the decks; they were very dirty for there was no water with which to wash. In the wardroom we had enough to wash our hands and faces once every day, but that was all. A little wine was carried for the officers. The food consisted chiefly of sausage, which was served at every meal, and canned bread and lard, which they called marmalade. Remy told me, however, that the crews on the submarines were the only people in Germany who had an unlimited amount of meat and other foods.

We had practically four meals every day: breakfast at 8 a. m., dinner at noon, and at 4 p. m. what they called '*kaffee*'; at 8 p. m. we had supper but practically every meal was the same. *Kaffee* at 4 p. m. apparently corresponded to our tea, but the sausage, or as they called it '*wurst*' was placed on the table at every meal. After supper we played cards, sometimes bridge and sometimes a new game which I was taught.

Captain Remy tried in every possible way to make things pleasant for me and whenever I asked him an impossible question, that is a question which he thought he ought not to answer, he invariably said so, so that I have great confidence that what he told me was the truth.

The *U-90* and most of the German submarines were out usually not more than four or five weeks and then in port about six or seven weeks. The service was not severe, for Remy got leave as often as he cared to have it and indeed it was deemed the height of good fortune by the regular officers to be assigned to a submarine. After making three round trips they were entitled to the iron cross and to leave, which leave covered the duration of the stay of the submarine in port. They received extra money and they got the best food in Germany, besides which for every day which they submerged both officers and men received extra money. For all these reasons the submarine service was very popular.

Lieutenant Isaacs had many interesting and harrowing experiences in German prison camps. Shortly after he had been taken off the submarine and placed in prison, he was summoned before the commander of the base, who immediately asked him why America had declared war. This under ordinary conditions is a rather difficult question to answer, not because there was a lack of reasons, but because in order to answer it well, a certain amount of thought is necessary. Lieutenant Isaacs apparently believed that any thought on the matter would be wasted and so informed the German Admiral that America had declared war because the American people thought the German people so many swine.

From then on things did not go very well with Lieutenant Isaacs. He was transferred to a prison camp from which he escaped, and was arrested. While *en route* to another prison camp he jumped out of the train window and landed on his head on the railroad bed. The train stopped and though he had regained consciousness from his fall, he was forced to surrender to the German soldiers when they began shooting at him. He was then kicked all the way to the next town, a distance of about nine miles. He planned another escape from the next camp and so was transferred again. Here, in making plans for a third attempt to escape, he found that Russian prisoners were acting as informants for the camp authorities.

He confided in a few English and Americans, and according to prearranged plans, one night, a good many of them escaped by short-circuiting the lighting system of the camp. He then walked for three nights, hiding during the day, to the Swiss border, and swam the Rhine. In Switzerland he reported to the American Consul, who informed Admiral Sims and Isaacs was ordered to Paris and then to London. He arrived in London about ten days later, very much undaunted in spirit and apparently not much the worse for the treatment he had received in the German prison camps.

CHAPTER 10

The Destruction of Submarines

One phase of the submarine war, which was very much misunderstood by the civilian, was the destruction of submarines. The many unreliable stories of the sinkings of submarines by merchant ships and patrol vessels have given people the idea that submarines were comparatively easy vessels to sink. As a matter of fact, in this war the submarine was the most difficult of any vessel to sink, and statistics show that only one submarine was sunk in every thirty-nine attempts to destroy it. One reason for this was the construction of the submarine itself; it was made in such a way that it had an outer and an inner hull, the space between which was used for carrying fuel. These fuel tanks served as buffers against any shock or force with which the submarine might come in contact, and though the hull might be tortioned slightly, the average submarine seemed capable of surviving all sorts of difficulties.

Shortly after America declared war, we read in the newspapers that the S. S. *Mongolia* had destroyed a submarine on the first shot; and a little later we read that the first troop convoy to France, when attacked by seven submarines, had managed to demolish most of them. On neither occasion was a sinking effected. There were two things in encounters with submarines which led the uninitiated erroneously to believe that a submarine had been destroyed: one was a large cloud of smoke, which would be seen rising from the water where the U-boat had submerged; the other was the oil and bubbles which would come to the surface after an attack. Both phenomena are easily explained.

I have said that when a submarine was on the surface, the Diesel oil engines were used as means of propulsion. These oil engines had an exhaust pipe and manifold not unlike that of an automobile. When a shell was fired at a submarine on the surface, it would immediately submerge, and as it did so cold water would rush into the hot exhaust pipe. In a moment steam would be formed inside the exhaust pipe, and as soon as a sufficiently powerful pocket of this had been generated, the water would be blown out of the manifold with great force, and with it would go all sorts of carbon gases, causing a small geyser of steam, water, and smoke. Thus, the gunner who had fired a shell at a submarine was led to believe that his shell, if it came anywhere near the submarine, had damaged it as proved by the smoke and water jet.

"Oil and bubbles" was taken at first as another proof that a submarine had been destroyed; it was in reality nothing of the sort. A submarine is an oily affair anywhere, and when it submerged it often left an oil patch on the surface. This might be caused by the exhaust explosion already mentioned, or by a small leak in a fuel tank; or it might be due to the fact that the commanding officer had deliberately discharged some oil out through the side of the submarine to make the attackers think that their work was finished, and so leave it alone.

There were three excellent ways of knowing when a submarine had been sunk. The surest way and most satisfactory to all concerned was by rescuing a few half-drowned survivors, who had managed to crawl out of the submarine through the conning tower, or through the torpedo tubes, when it was far below the surface, and going down rapidly. The capture of survivors under any circumstances was good proof that a submarine had been destroyed. Another method was by observing on the charts, as kept by the radio direction finder, whether a submarine after an attack continued to operate or not.

If a vessel attacked a submarine, and during the following night that submarine communicated with Germany by wireless, there was excellent proof that the submarine had not been sunk. On the other hand, if a patrol vessel attacked a submarine and no further movements were observed, it might be supposed that it had been sunk. Whether it had been sunk or not remained to be seen, and this introduces the third way, namely, whether it ever returned to its base. This information would be supplied by the English secret agents in Germany and neutral countries, although it was often weeks and months before definite word could be obtained.

For example, the U. S. S. *Lydonia* and H. M. S. *Basilisk* dropped depth charges on a submarine in the Mediterranean on May 8, 1918, and in submitting their reports the commanding officers of these vessels did not even claim to have destroyed it. No further movements of this submarine were recorded, but credit for its destruction was not awarded until August, when the Admiralty, by checking up all information from their agents and charts learned that it had not returned to its base at Pola, classified it as "sunk."

This aversion on the part of the Admiralty and later on the part of Admiral Sims and his associates, to consider a submarine sunk when absolute proof thereof was lacking, was warranted. I have said that the German Intelligence Service often allowed the wish to father the thought, and showed how such methods were detrimental. In order to combat the submarine, all operations had to be based upon a knowledge of facts; therefore, marking off a submarine as sunk before its destruction was definitely proven, was misleading and not a good policy. If as many submarines had been sunk as were claimed, Germany would have had to have built about five thousand of them.

As it was, the Admiralty, knew from day to day and from week to week, because of the conservative policy in estimating submarine losses, exactly how many German submarines were available for service at all times, and at future dates. As great as was the desire on the part of the officials to classify these as sunk, a false representation of their destruction would have helped nobody but the Germans themselves.

Statistics show that the most effective method of sinking submarines was by depth charges. These explosive weapons were a new invention in Naval Warfare, and were first used in the autumn of 1916. Previous to that time the anti-submarine vessel had had no offensive weapon against a submerged submarine. The introduction of the depth charge altered and improved the situation. The depth charge was similar in appearance and size to a hogshead, and was filled with explosives. At one end of these "cans," as they were affectionately called by the members of the destroyer force, there was a mechanism similar to that of a time fuse on a shell. This mechanism was so delicate that at various depths, according to the adjustment, the water pressure on it would cause the explosion.

Depth charges were carried on the stern of the vessel on an oiled track or runway, from which they could be easily launched into the water. There was also a depth-charge thrower, known as the "Y" gun, by which they could be heaved 200 yards to either side of the vessel. The force of the explosion under water was so great that it was absolutely imperative for the destroyer to be going at full speed when they were being dropped, to avoid being herself injured. A depth charge, exploding within 50 yards of a submarine, would have the effect of pushing almost a solid mass (water under sudden impact acts practically as a solid), against the side of the submarine, tending to crush it.

A depth-charge launching device on the stern of a destroyer.

Should the explosion occur beneath the submarine, it would find itself pushed toward the surface, or tilted up on end, all of which would probably be injurious to it. It often happened that the explosion would injure the diving or elevating apparatus, corresponding to a horizontal rudder on the submarine, and in such cases it would either find itself rapidly rising to the surface or rapidly going down.

When a destroyer sighted a submarine, she would steam at full speed towards the point where it was seen, or as near to such a position as could be determined, and the "cans" would be dropped. When they were first used, and during 1917, it was the custom to drop only two or three and some very excellent results were obtained; notably the sinking of a submarine by the *Fanning* and the injuring of a submarine by the *Christabel*. But though submarines had been sunk and injured in this way, a few of the authorities, and Admiral Sims in particular, advocated a change in tactics. Admiral Sims rightly believed that the greater the number of depth charges dropped, the better the chances of success. He also believed that the occurrence of many severe explosions would tend to frighten the crew of a submarine, and demoralise them.

In March, 1918, he sent instructions to all his forces that five depth charges were to be dropped in the future for every one dropped in the past. This system proved very effective, and although the destruction of submarines thereby was not materially increased, it undoubtedly wrought havoc with the personnel of the submarines. When a submarine was attacked, and the terrible explosions began to occur all around it, the crew at times became almost panic stricken; lights would go out, sometimes leaks would occur, all storage batteries be upset, and in general, the crew would experience a few very exasperating moments, all of which tended towards killing their "nerve" and increasing their fear of destroyers. In this way the U-boats became more cautious in revealing themselves; and more caution on the part of the submarines meant fewer Allied losses.

According to this new method, fifteen or twenty, or sometimes as many as thirty depth charges were dropped at the slightest provocation. Dropping them was easy enough; the question was where to drop them. A submarine sighted at a given point, would be able to move only a certain distance within a given time; in other words, it would be inside a circle, the size of which would be determined by the length of time intervening between the sighting of the submarine and the arrival of the destroyer at the point where it was seen. As

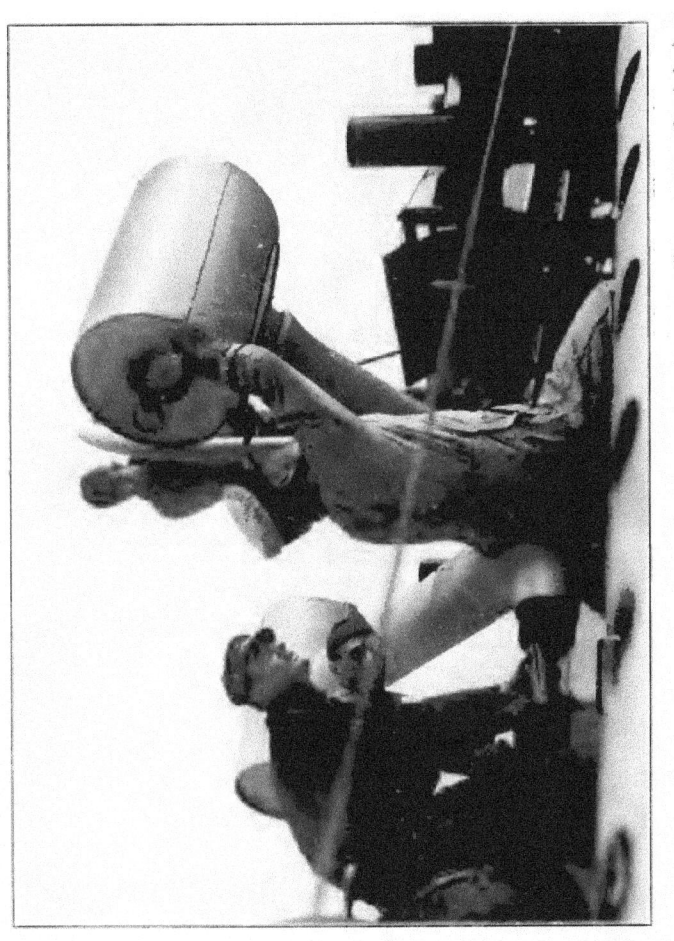

The "Y" gun by which depth charges could be heaved sideways. The man on the left is loading the gun, and the one on the right is adjusting the mechanism which determined at what depth the "can" exploded.

the speed of a submerged U-boat was known, it could be calculated within what area it must be. When the destroyer arrived at the position where the submarine was seen, she would commence to drop depth charges in a circle having a radius in proportion to the time consumed in describing it.

Thus, if a destroyer started to describe a circle towards the right, as she continued the circle, the rudder would be eased, and the radius would be increased until it overlapped at the point from which it was started. In dropping these charges, the destroyer was confronted with the problem as to the depth at which they should be set to explode. Some submarines submerged to thirty feet when attacked, others to 200, and the destroyer's officer had no means of knowing which. It was anybody's guess.

In spite of the best possible mathematical and scientific calculations hundreds of depth charges were dropped without results, except for the usual oil and bubbles which meant nothing, and the nerve-racking explosions which the submarine crews experienced. As Commander Cook, U. S. N., commanding officer of the U. S. Destroyer *Allen*, once said:

> You can give me all the science in the world, but when you have sighted a submarine and steamed a mile to reach the point where it submerged, I defy you to know when or where to begin to drop your depth charges and at what depth to set them. The submarine may be anywhere inside an area of several hundred yards and may be 30 feet or 200 feet below the surface. Nevertheless, I throw as many 'cans' overboard, as I dare, at the slightest provocation; and though I have not bagged one yet I have made things unpleasant for many.

The American forces delivered 286 attacks on submarines or on suspicious objects; in 197 of these, it was definitely proved that a submarine was present. The remaining attacks were carried out upon oil slicks on the water, or tide rips, or some other form of disturbance. The reports of attacks were sent by the commanding officer of the vessels involved to Admiral Sims' office in London, and, upon the receipt of these, a comparison of the position in which the attack was delivered with the current charts of submarine movements was made. In this way it was known how effective and successful the attacks had been.

Four submarines were sunk by the American forces, one on November 27, 1917, by the U. S. S. *Fanning* and *Nicholson*; another on

May 11, 1918, by the U. S. S. *Lydonia*, in the Mediterranean; a third on June 18 by the submarine chasers at Corfu; and the fourth on October 2, 1918, by the chasers at Corfu in their raid on Durazzo Harbour. A fifth was possibly sunk by the U. S. S. *Tucker* on August 8, 1918, a hundred miles off Brest, and on May 31st the *Christabel* attacked the *UC-56* and forced it to intern at Santander, Spain. It is possible and probable that the American forces sank other submarines also, but as the same thing is true of the British, French, and Italian Forces, it was decided that, in order to avoid any argument over the crediting of these sinkings to various nations, it would be better to classify those cases where the time and cause of destruction were not definitely proven, as "means of sinking unknown."

In 17 other attacks, American vessels were successful to the extent that in these encounters, submarines were slightly or seriously damaged, and forced, because of injuries, to return to their bases immediately. The vessels participating in these attacks were as follows:

Trippe
  July 9, 1917
Wadsworth
  July 21, 1917
Benham
  July 30, 1917
McDougal
  September 9, 1917
Noma ⎫
Wakiva ⎬ Nov. 28, 1917
Kanawha ⎪
Patterson ⎫
Beale ⎬ May 19, 1918
Burrows ⎪
Allen ⎭
Warrington
  July 13, 1917
Wilkes
  July 26, 1917

Parker
  August 3, 1917
Davis
  September 21, 1917
Allen
  February 2, 1918
Jenkins
  July 17, 1917
Wadsworth & Trippe
  July 29, 1917
Jacob Jones
  September 5, 1917

Porter
  April 28, 1918
Sterrett
  June 1, 1918
Sub-Chasers, Plymouth
  July 10, 1918

CHAPTER 11

Why American Troopships were Not Sunk

When America declared war in 1917 the thought immediately occurred to us, "How are we going to send troops to France with submarines blocking the path?" While we were pondering over this, the Germans were gloating and saying, "Americans will never get to France; our submarines will stop them." The long and short of our wondering and Germany's gloating was that our troops did get to France, with but few casualties. Why were there no serious losses of transports and men? To this question I am going to undertake an answer on my own responsibility. I believe that the Germans did not make a determined effort to sink American transports. This statement may seem startling at first, but a closer study of the matter will show that from a military point of view it was a better policy for submarines not to try to stop American troops coming to France.

The original conception of the submarine war involved primarily the blockade of Great Britain, and thereby the subsequent starvation of the Allies by sinking British cargo vessels. Sinking American troops was not starving England, and every time a torpedo was fired at a transport, there was one torpedo less to be used in the destruction of ships carrying food to England. The Germans knew that we had limitless numbers of men whom we could send to France; what was to be gained by sinking a few of these when there were just as many more to come?

In order to prevent American troops landing in Europe, the submarines would have had to devote their entire attention, energy, and practically all their torpedoes to sinking transports. Such a policy would not have been in accord with the original doctrine of the U-boat campaign, which was, as stated, to starve England by sinking cargo vessels. They could not sink both; their efforts had to be concentrated on one or on the other. There were excellent reasons for not concentrating their efforts on transports.

I have already shown how the sinking of a fast ship on a zigzag course, protected by destroyers, was an exceedingly difficult task for a submarine. A submarine, in manoeuvring to get close enough to a fast zigzagging vessel to fire a torpedo at her, was putting itself in a very dangerous position; and at that, the chances of a torpedo striking its mark, because of the speed and irregular course of the target, were not too good. And after the torpedo had been fired, there were half a dozen destroyers ready to pounce upon the submarine with depth charges, and if it was not destroyed or injured, the submarine itself and its crew would spend a very dangerous and uncomfortable fifteen minutes.

In other words, attacking fast ships, such as troopships, when well protected by destroyers, was almost too dangerous to the submarine to be worthwhile. The commanding officer undoubtedly appreciated the pleasures of being alive, and though his superior back in Germany probably did not care what his sentiments were on this matter, he nevertheless did not want to lose the use of the submarine—which meant the saving of 20,000 tons per month to the Allies. It is only natural that the officer in command of the flotillas did not want to lose the use of a submarine by its endeavouring to sink a transport, when sinking a transport would be of little military value, and not in accord with the primary doctrine of the submarine campaign.

Admiral von Capelle, who was Chief of the Submarine Service, undoubtedly realised this, and apparently did not order his submarines to devote their efforts towards sinking American troops. His good sense cost him his position, for in July, 1918, when it became known that many American troops had reached France, he was forced to resign. Nevertheless, his successor. Admiral von Mann, probably realised that Von Capelle was right, for only one transport was sunk after the first of August.

The next question is how many transports were sunk, and do their losses prove or disapprove my theory? Six were sunk, and two more were definitely attacked. The vessels sunk were the U. S. Army Transport *Antilles*, the British S. S. *Moldavia*, the H. M. S. *Tuscania*, and the U. S. S. *President Lincoln*; also, the H. M. S. *Justicia* and the U. S. S. *Covington*. The U. S. S. *Mt. Vernon* was torpedoed, but she made port, and the *Olympic* accidentally rammed a submarine which was contemplating an attack. The first four of these cases, in that these ships resembled cargo vessels in general appearance, cannot be regarded in the same category as the others. Let us take each case individually.

The *Antilles* was sunk in the summer of 1917, while proceeding back to this country. She was an old coastwise vessel of small tonnage with but one stack and not much deck structure; in other words, she was not a liner in appearance. The *Tuscania* was torpedoed and sunk off the North Coast of Ireland in February, 1918. At the time of her destruction, she was lagging behind a slow merchant convoy at dusk, and in her general appearance she was not unlike the vessels she was following. Invariably experience has shown that the vessel which lagged behind has been the one selected for destruction by the submarine.

The third case is that of the *Moldavia*, which was sunk in the English Channel while carrying American troops from England to France. This vessel was originally a cargo carrier, and during the war had been converted into a refrigerator ship. She was fundamentally a cargo vessel, and it was merely a coincidence that she had American troops on board when destroyed. The fourth case was that of the *President Lincoln*, which was sunk on May 30, 1918, three hundred miles West of Brest.

This ship was an old German combination cargo and passenger (second class only) carrier; she had one stack and six masts, with many hoists and derricks for loading purposes. To all appearances she was a cargo vessel. In fact, all four of these ships were either cargo vessels or very similar to them, the only exception perhaps being the *Tuscania*, but she was torpedoed at dusk when lagging behind a cargo convoy. The loss of these vessels, does not prove that the Germans were making a determined effort to sink transports.

Two transports which could not be taken for cargo vessels, the *Justicia* and the *Covington*, were sunk, and two more, the *Mt. Vernon* and the *Olympic* were attacked.

★★★★★★★★★★

Incidentally, the Press claimed that the *Justicia* had been sunk by four submarines, which was not true. On July 19, 1918, on the North Coast of Ireland at dusk, she was hit by a torpedo from a submarine, which was Northward bound. She remained afloat all night, and was being towed back to port when the following morning, another submarine Southward bound discovered her in this condition, and sank her.

★★★★★★★★★★

The reason for torpedoing these vessels was probably the same as that for sinking hospital ships. It is a well-known fact that submarines

The U. S. S. Covington, torpedoed July 4, 1918. She stayed afloat for sixteen hours, after being struck. This vessel and the U. S. S. President Lincoln were the only big U. S. troopships lost in the war.

sank hospital ships in order to make the Allies use destroyers in escorting them. I believe that the same is true in these cases, for as long as but few transports were being sunk, the Germans probably thought that the Allies might see fit to let them be unescorted. This would mean that an extra number of destroyers would be available for escorting cargo ships, which were the real prey of the submarine. By sinking an occasional transport or hospital ship, they could force the Allies to supply escorts to these vessels, and thereby have less destroyers available to protect cargo ships.

Now to sum up. I first showed that the sinking of transports was not the real object of the submarine war, and that attempts at their destruction in large numbers would have meant the abandonment of the real objective of the campaign, namely, the starvation of England by sinking cargo vessels. I then showed that because of the convoy system, attempts to sink transports were not worth the risk the submarine incurred in so doing. And then finally, I showed that those eight cases. In which transports were sunk or attached, did not prove that the enemy was making a determined effort to sink *troopships*; because, four of them were not transports in general appearance and because the other four, though unmistakably transports, were attacked in order to force the Allies to escort all troopships very heavily, and thereby leave fewer destroyers available for escort duty with *cargo* convoys.

This may lead the reader to conclude that our navy did not do such a great deal after all. Such a conclusion would be far from true, for insurance against Allied defeat lay *not* in making it possible to transport American soldiers to France, but *in checking* the submarines sufficiently to allow all Allied Europeans three good meals a day, and occasionally a lump of sugar. It has often been said that even if the German Army had overrun France, Germany would not have been victorious so long as the Allies commanded the sea.

While submarines were on the high-road to starving England, Germany, though she did not control the surface of the seas, possessed sufficient power under the surface to accomplish her desires. The Allies' salvation and gateway to success lay in feeding their peoples and armies. The slogan the "Navy brought 'em over" is of minor importance. What the navy did do was to keep the Allies and their armies from starving.

CHAPTER 12

The End of the Submarine Campaign

During the spring and summer of 1918, the sinkings by submarines steadily decreased; the Allied Navies had the situation well in hand. Of course, ships were sunk, and always would be, as long as there were submarines at sea, but the situation looked better, and the anti-submarine struggle promised greater success than at any other previous date. The British dockyards were launching greater numbers of new anti-submarine vessels, and every month brought more American destroyers to the theatre of war. The construction of German submarines was going on as before, and though their total was gradually increasing, their successes at sea were being steadily checked.

Another great factor, which gave encouragement to the Allied Naval Authorities, was the monthly construction of American Merchant tonnage, which, added to British new construction, surpassed the monthly losses. These facts produced the "handwriting on the wall "for the German submarine. The submarine became a weapon of power to Germany shortly after the outbreak of the war in 1914, and grew in danger as the war progressed. The Royal Navy kept the ravages on tonnage low as long as Germany carried on her submarine war according to international law, which Germany officially violated in February, 1917, when she informed the world that the waters East of the British Isles and France were "blockaded."

It is provided in international law that a nation at war may declare the enemy's ports blockaded, if such a blockade is effective. This means that warships of one nation may prevent the entrance of ships to the ports of the enemy by the right of search and seizure. Thus, if they stop an enemy merchant ship on the high seas, that vessel can be taken captive and made to return to its enemy's port. Or when the blockading vessel so decides, if the merchant ship is carrying contraband, the cargo can be seized and the vessel sunk or captured. In the case of a neutral, the cargo, if determined contraband, can be seized or destroyed, but the vessel cannot be captured or sunk. Thus, England's blockade of Germany in this war was permissible according to international law, for it could be enforced according to international law.

English warships could, and did, prevent American vessels carrying contraband into Germany, directly or indirectly, through neutral countries. British war vessels would stop American vessels, which were neutral, remove the contraband, and allow the vessel to proceed. England's blockade of Germany was effective. When Germany declared all waters three hundred miles East of England and France "blockaded," her declaration and its execution were illegal because it could not be effectively carried out according to international law. Germany, to blockade England, could only use submarines. If submarines had stopped neutral vessels, seized or destroyed the cargo and then allowed the ship to proceed, their actions would have been legitimate; but as submarines in English waters could not stop and search ships without encountering British warships, this was impossible.

Also, if a submarine had been able to stop British ships and take them back to Germany as captures, or after search, have sunk them, their actions would have been legitimate. But because submarines could not, and did not, do these two things, Germany violated international law, both in her declaration of a blockade because it was not totally effective and because in its execution her submarines sank the vessels of England and neutral countries on sight without warning. This violation of international law, and the high-handed disregard with which Germany treated the vessels of neutrals, brought America at last into the great struggle.

At the time of America's entry into the war, England's tonnage losses through submarines were greater than that nation could long stand, and her auxiliary naval vessels—*viz.*, destroyers, gun-boats etc., were not sufficient in numbers to serve with the Grand Fleet which had the German Fleet bottled up in the North Sea and at the same time combat the submarine in all areas. The American Navy, under the command of Admiral Sims, upon its arrival in European waters, extended a willing and helping hand in a spirit of unprecedented cooperation to the hard-pressed British and other Allied Navies. Thirty destroyers joined the British Forces at Queenstown and were employed in protecting shipping to and from England in the waters South of Ireland.

At Brest, forty-one destroyers, some yachts, and mine-sweepers co-

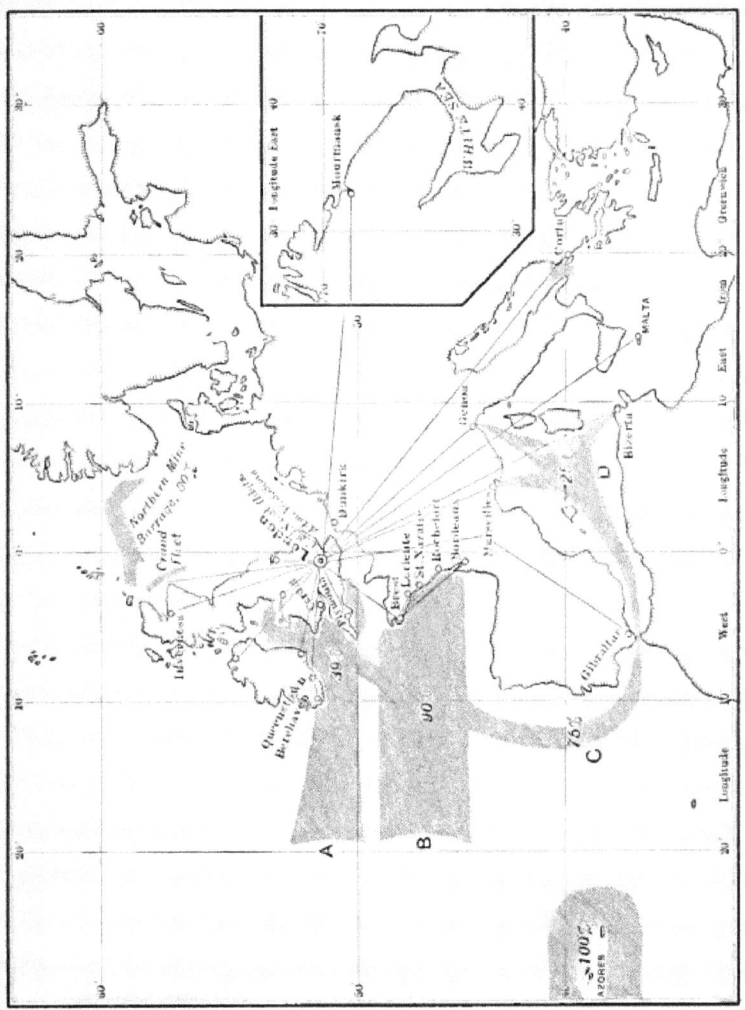

The shaded areas show the areas in which our forces operated; the borders of the shaded parts are general, and they do not mean that American forces remained inside them. The figures show the percentages of traffic, escorted by American naval vessels. The lines running in all directions show how Admiral Sims was in communication with all of his bases.

operated with the French and undertook whatever duty arose. At Gibraltar, thirty-five American vessels joined with the British vessels in escorting local Mediterranean convoys and convoys between Gibraltar and Great Britain. Five American dreadnoughts joined the British Fleet in the North Sea and three others made their base at Berehaven in the role of an offensive squadron against possible enemy raiders. The American Mine Force in Scotland laid 80%, or 56,000 mines, of the Northern Mine Barrage from Scotland to Norway, the greatest mining operation in history. American chasers operated around the island of Corfu and maintained a constant watch at the mouth of the Adriatic where all enemy submarines in the Mediterranean had their base. Another detachment of chasers was stationed at Plymouth, and remained on constant patrol in the English Channel.

A third squadron of chasers arrived at Queenstown, but the Armistice cut short their activities. An American cruiser was dispatched to Archangel; seventy-three American cargo vessels, manned by naval personnel, carried coal from Cardiff, Wales, to France for the use of the American Expeditionary Force. The American Naval Aviation Service established twenty-nine stations and schools along the Coasts of France, England, Ireland, and Italy. Thus with 374 vessels, which steamed an average of 626,000 miles per month, with a complement of 78,000 men, the American Naval Forces shouldered a good proportion of the war against the submarine. In the Eastern Atlantic, our destroyers provided about 27% of the escorts to convoys.

★★★★★★★★★★

The Royal Navy provided 70% of the escorts, the American 27%, and the French 3%. The actual number of Allied war vessels employed in the war was over 4,000; of these we furnished but 374. It will be well for the American people to recognise in this way the great ability of Admiral Sims. His Forces were the fewest in number of any great power in this war, and yet look at what he accomplished with them.

★★★★★★★★★★

The acute stage of the submarine campaign passed with the introduction of the convoy system in July, 1917. By January, 1918, it was made clear to all, except the propaganda-nourished German population, that the submarine was not to bring defeat to the Allies. Perhaps by 1918 the German Naval Officials realised that their submarines could not bring their country victory, but in order to defend themselves for their acts, which cost Germany the price of active American participation in the war, and in order to hamper the Allies as much

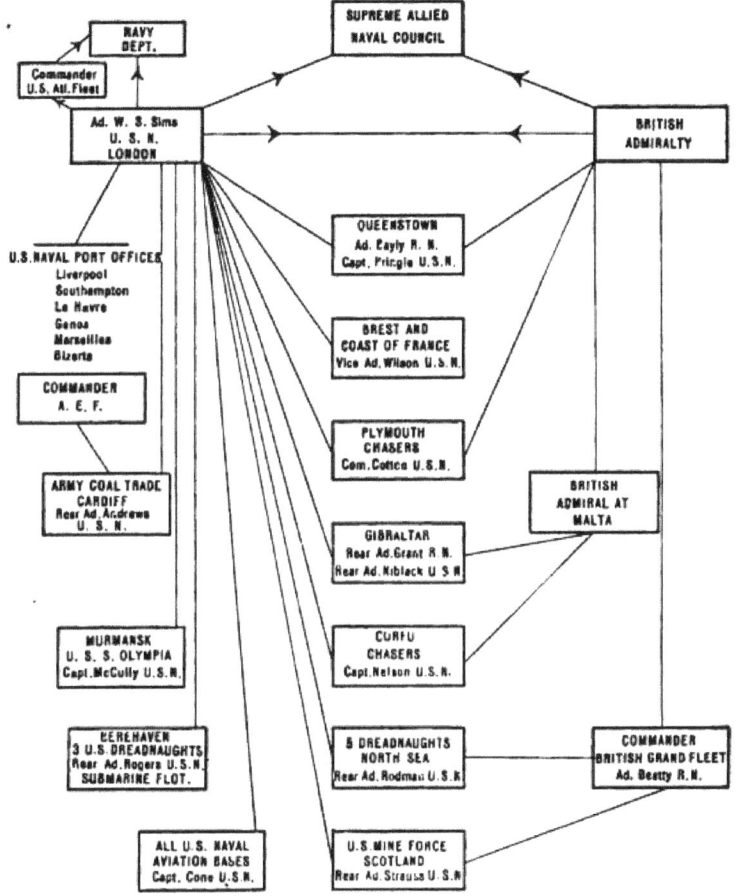

A graphic representation of Admiral Sims' version of "Unity of Command." The joining lines show the cooperation between the high authorities and the bases.

as possible, the submarine war was continued. Great yarns were given out in Germany about the success of the submarine campaign, but these coincided with the stories of what the submarines would do, rather than with what they really did. But there is no denying that the submarine, until September, 1918, remained a strong weapon in the hands of Germany and that the U-boat war was pressed with great virulence until almost the very end.

The beginning of the end of the submarine war made itself apparent in September, 1918. During that month the sinkings amounted to only 180,000 tons, a fact occasioned through the loss of morale of the submarine crews, perhaps partially the result of a clever move by the British Admiralty. In August, the Admiralty made public a list of the names of 150 submarine commanders who had been lost, and all of whose submarines had been destroyed. This information showed the existing submarine commanders that the British Admiralty knew considerably more of their activities than was supposed.

How the British and Admiral Sims kept themselves informed of submarine activities, the Germans never discovered, for the *Kaiser's* Intelligence office never learned the secret of locating submarines by wireless. When it became evident to the submarine officers and crews that their every movement was watched by the British Admiralty, greater caution on their part was manifested, and the daring which had characterized their operations disappeared.

The proof that the British Admiralty knew a great deal more about submarine operations than was commonly supposed came to the German submarine personnel as a letter does to a man informing him that his bank-account has been overdrawn. The men and officers began to think, and soon probably appreciated the following facts.

The German Admiralty had said in February, 1917, that the war would be over by the autumn. This statement had not come true. The American Navy had come into the war, and by efficient cooperation with the British, for many a submarine officer had seen English and American destroyers with the same convoy, had increased the difficulty of the submarine's task. Also, the convoy system had made the destruction of a ship by a submarine an extremely difficult and hazardous task. And every time they went to sea, they had to encounter a great danger, the Northern Mine Barrage, because the still greater danger, the Dover mine-fields, had closed the Straits to them. And when at sea, their encounters with Allied patrol craft were ever growing more numerous. Their mortal enemy had sunk over 150 submarines and ap-

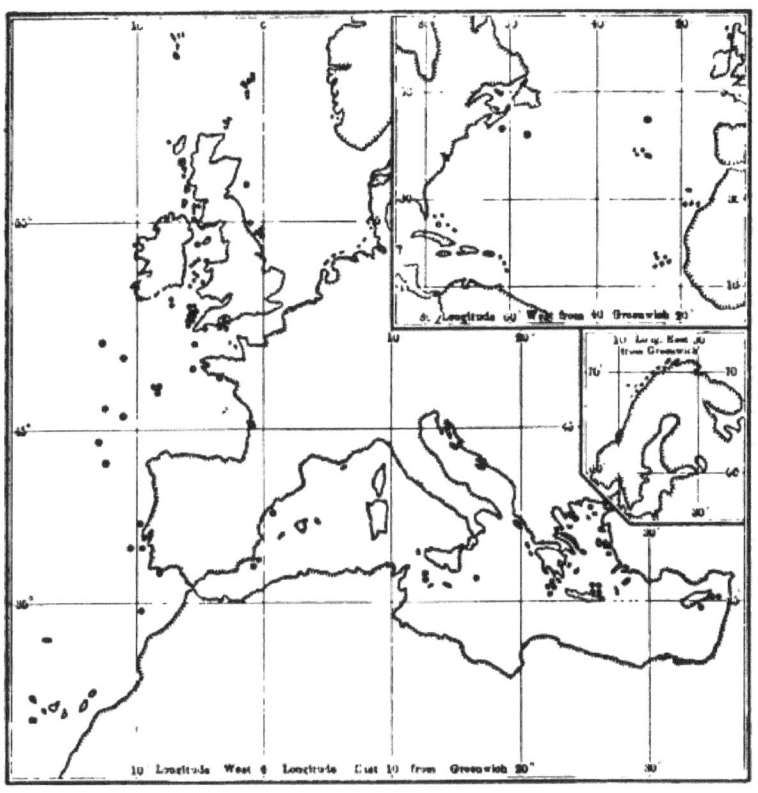

The little dots represent the Allied vessels sunk by submarines in September, 1918; five or six dots in place of each of these would represent the losses of April, 1917. The two ships sunk off our coast (see insert) were destroyed by the U-117, the last of the four German submarines to visit our coasts.

parently watched the activities of every submarine commander with intelligence and interest.

And, finally, in spite of their efforts, the Allied tonnage losses were being more than replaced by new construction, although there were more submarines ready for operations than ever before. To what hopes could they now turn? Or what could they accomplish by continuing to play a game in which they had no hopes and in which their comrades in arms, the German Armies were playing a losing part?

Such sentiments on the part of the submarine crews were not revealed to the Allied Naval authorities except by the actions of the submarines themselves. During the last week of September submarine operations became confused, and the following of each submarine difficult; activities seemed to lack proper guidance. The sinkings decreased notably during that month, and by October, the impression was gathered that the submarines were trying to conceal themselves as much as possible. By the middle of October, after the commencement of rumours of an Armistice, many submarines started for home, and attacks on merchant ships became scarce. By the end of October, only half a dozen were still operating. This sudden collapse of the submarine war served as an excellent barometer of the coming debacle.

By the first week in November, the seas were practically cleared of submarines. The efforts of the British Naval authorities and Admiral Sims had been successful. The U-boat war, by their efforts, had failed. But these men, in their hour of success, gave way to no jubilation. They continued the anti-submarine tactics, as if the submarines were operating as in past months. Who knew but that Germany, in her death-rattle, might send her 174 submarines, the greatest number she had ever had, to sea, with orders to sink everything afloat? Who knew but that this might be her last effort, in her dying gasp? The dying gasp came a few days later, but in another form, when the High Seas Fleet was ordered to sea. Mutiny followed, and no German warship left its anchorage.

Two weeks later, the High Seas Fleet and the submarines surrendered. After an examination of the German warships, it was learned that for two and a half years, the German Navy had been in no condition to meet the British. The German Naval authorities had apparently decided, after the Battle of Jutland, in June, 1916, that their navy was no match for the English Navy in open combat. They then had turned to the submarine to fulfil their ambition for Naval supremacy. In this, too, they had failed, and Germany was beaten at a game of her

Among those who officiated at the surrender of the German Fleet were, left to right, Admiral Beatty, R. N., Rear Admiral Rodman, U. S. N., King George V, the Prince of Wales, and Admiral Sims, on the deck of the U. S. S. New York.

own choosing. When the first group of German submarines surrendered, Germany unwillingly admitted before the world that England
and America ruled not only the surface of the sea, but also controlled
what Germany had seen fit to stage beneath it.

CHAPTER 13

The Man on the Bridge (in Homage)

In 1775 John Paul Jones, the Father of the American Navy, in a letter to Congress, described at length the requirements of intellect and character necessary to a naval officer of the highest order. Among other things he said:

> It is by no means enough that an officer of the navy should be a capable mariner. He must be that, of course, but also a great deal more. He should be as well, a gentleman of liberal education, refined manners, punctilious courtesy, and have the nicest sense of personal honour. He should also be conversant with the uses of diplomacy, and capable of maintaining, if called upon, a dignified and judicious correspondence (which means position); because it often happens that sudden emergencies in foreign waters make him the diplomatic as well as the military representative of his country.—These are the general qualifications, and the nearer the officer approaches the full possession of them, the more likely he will be to serve our country well, and win fame and honour for himself.

The extracts in this summary are brief but satisfactory and we all agree that John Paul Jones had a splendid vision of the duties of a naval officer.

When standards of this sort are set, it is not often that we find them fulfilled, for they are beyond the grasp of most men. Standards and ideals are human institutions to be constantly striven after, but seldom attained. They owe their origin to the accomplishments and character of one man whose life, or life's work, is passed along as the goal towards which other men should strive. John Paul Jones probably realised that his version of the ideal naval officer was not to be attained by many, but some day might be reached by a few. Admirals Farragut and Dewey have lived up to his standards in the past, and today the same may be said of Rear-Admiral William Snowden Sims.

This officer, because of his absence in Europe for two years and his besetting sin, modesty, is not so well known to the American people as is his due. This is to a large extent his own fault, for his modesty and dislike of ceremony have deprived him of that fame which others less modest have attained. At our naval offices in London, there was a newspaper man attached to the staff as the central correspondent of our Forces in Europe. This officer saw that as much information, as could be made public about the American Naval activities abroad was sent back to this country.

Information of every sort except that concerning Admiral Sims was given out. All material for the American Press had to be passed upon by the admiral, and whenever articles dealing with himself were submitted for approval, they were rejected. Again, and again this newspaper correspondent went to the admiral, personally, and asked him to allow stories of himself to be sent to the American Press; and as often as this was asked, just so often would Admiral Sims reply:

Let's cut out this talk, and get on with the war; after the war there will be lots of time for talking.

This was his method of doing things, and it permeated his whole character.

Very nearly every staff officer in this war, above the rank of major, was allowed the use of a staff automobile. American generals in this country and in France and the general commanding our troops in England, all had their own staff cars, marked with insignia of their rank. This was not the case with Admiral Sims. At his headquarters in London there were 196 officers, who had at their disposal five staff cars and each one was modestly marked "U. S. N." One of these cars was reserved for the admiral's use during the day, but if he was not going to use it for an hour or two, it was at the disposal of any officer. At night all cars were dismissed shortly after six o'clock, and the admiral, as an ordinary citizen, would walk or take a bus back to his room at the Carlton Hotel.

Of course, he was entertained officially on many occasions, and at all of these functions he was usually the principal speaker. He is the possessor of a ready wit and is full of humorous stories gained by extensive reading on all subjects. He is exceedingly well informed, and because his comprehension of facts and his interpretations of cause

ADMIRAL WILLIAM SNOWDEN SIMS.

and result are very keen, he never fails to see the humorous side of life and history. Socially he was also entertained, but he considered generally that such affairs could wait. He limited his social activities as much as possible to small dinners in private houses where the atmosphere was one of friendliness and congeniality rather than that of a social affair. He believed that as long as there was a war on, the great task with which he was confronted should in no way be interrupted by matters not pertinent to his work. He was always on the bridge.

Because of his "liberal education, refined manners, punctilious courtesy, and the nicest sense of personal honour," he soon was looked upon as a diplomatic representative of America, as well as the Commander of our Forces. His ability as a speaker, his gentle voice and dignity, all went to make him unconsciously diplomatically important. It will be recalled that in the spring of 1918, Mr. Page, our Ambassador to the Court of St. James, returned to this country because of ill health, and for several months thereafter his position was vacant. In the Fall of that year, talk concerning the choice of the new Ambassador being prevalent, a Member of Parliament made the remark;

> As long as Admiral Sims is here, your country does not need an ambassador.

This remark was to the point, and though the admiral of course did not become involved in state affairs, nevertheless to the layman and citizen of London, America and Admiral Sims were synonymous. His cooperation and diplomatic conduct in dealings with the Admiralty and chiefs of other Allied organisations, made a deep impression on British public opinion. The tale was popularly told that he came to loggerheads with the Admiralty one day when, after the king had bestowed upon him the honorary title of "Knight Commander of the most holy Order of St. Michael and St. George," a British officer at the Admiralty greeted him as "Sir William."

Admiral Sims did a great deal to cement that much desired "Anglo-American Unity." I recall one day in January when our recently appointed ambassador, Mr. Davis, was being entertained at the American Luncheon Club. The Right Hon. Mr. Balfour gave a little talk, in the course of which he said:

> I know that the Englishman has little peculiarities all his own; for instance, an Englishman always walks into a drawing room as if it belonged to him.

The admiral was the next speaker, and thus he began:

In connection with what the Right Hon. Mr. Balfour has just said, I have a few words to say, for the American also has little peculiarities of his own, for whereas the Englishman walks into a room as if it belonged to *him*, the American usually walks in as if it belonged to *nobody*.

Quips such as these from the admiral at a time when ill winds bore to European ears the cry (in poor taste,) "America won the war," were usual, and time and time again, he would tactfully crash through the atmosphere of formality, and send everybody home with a firm conviction that if Admiral Sims represented the typical American, England and America were at heart similar.

Perhaps the incident which shows his great and sincere spirit most clearly, was his return to this country. I have tried to show the position he held in Europe. He had come to England at a very critical time. He had been received, respected, and praised for his services, and his position in London had been such as few foreigners have attained. He had ably commanded our navy in European Waters, and had sat as a conspicuous figure in the Supreme Allied Naval Council, and was the first Allied chief to establish real cooperation and unity of command. In view of this, the Navy Department had promoted him to the rank of temporary admiral; but according to naval regulations, an admiral, unless his rank is permanent, becomes a rear-admiral when he relinquishes his command.

Accordingly, Admiral Sims was a full admiral up to the time he left England. As the *Mauretania*, on which he returned, came up the harbour, amidst the waving of flags, blowing of whistles, and other emblems of welcome, the great hatches or doors in the side of the ship swung open, and there stood the man who had commanded our navy so capably, in the uniform of a rear-admiral.

Today his rank is still that of a rear-admiral, The President, and the Secretary of the Navy, have both recommended to Congress that he be promoted to the rank of permanent admiral; up to the present writing this has not been done. In Europe, men who in this war played a lesser part than Admiral Sims have been rewarded for their services by their governments. Rear-Admiral Sims, U. S. N., a naval officer, a diplomat, a gentleman, and a servant of his country, deserves the best his government can give him. His country has already given him the affection and that admiration he so richly deserves.

Appendix

The total number of submarines destroyed during the war was 203; this figure includes eight which were forced to intern because of injuries received in encounters with patrol vessels. The following table gives the methods by which they were destroyed:

Rammed by Man of War	4
" " Destroyer and Patrol Vessels	9
" " Merchant Vessels	4
Sunk by gunfire—Destroyer and Patrol Vessels	12
" " " Decoy Ship (Mystery Ship)	11
" " " Armed Smack	1
" " Depth Charges from Destroyer & Patrol Vessels	35
" " Allied mine-fields	34
" " Allied Submarines	17
" " Allied Submarine coöperating with a decoy ship	2
" " Aircraft	7
Blown up	14
Sunk by Accident	4
" " Collision with Enemy vessels	2
Stranded	3
Sunk by Mine-nets—moored	1
" " " " towed	8
" " Mines laid by Germany	5
" " Collision with paravane on Destroyer	3
" " Modified sweep	1
" " Bomb	1
Interned	8
Method of sinking unidentified	17
Total	203

It will be noted from this list that depth charges were the most effective weapon against the submarine; also, attention is called to the fact that 17 submarines were sunk by Allied submarines, and that none were sunk by merchant ship gunfire. Probably half of those sunk by unknown methods destroyed themselves through internal explosives or by getting caught on the bottom.

If we classify this list according to nationalities, we have sunk by :

British Vessels or British Mines	137
U.S. Vessels	4
French Vessels	3
Russian Vessels	2
	——
Total	146

The remaining boats were sunk by means other than a deliberate attack by Allied vessels, or by Allied operations.

The classification of this list according to the areas in which the submarines were sunk is interesting.

Sunk in the North Sea	86
" " " Dover Barrage	17
" " " English Channel	20
" " " Irish Sea	7
" " " Southwest of Ireland	7
" " " West of Ireland	1
" " " North of Ireland	5
" " " Northwest of Scotland	1
" " " Arctic Sea	3
" " " Baltic "	2
" " " Atlantic	4
" " " Black Sea	3
" " " Mediterranean	15
" " " Dardanelles	1
Interned in Spain	5
" " Holland	2
" " Norway	1
Blown up at bases—Flanders	4
" " Pola and Cattaro	10
Unidentified	6
	——
Total	200

It may seem strange that 17 submarines were destroyed by unknown means, and only 6 were destroyed in unknown places. This is easily explained, for submarines lying on the bottom have been found

143

when the cause of their destruction was unknown. The reader must not forget that practically all this information was in the hands of the authorities during the war. The accumulation of it was of great importance to the Allies while the war was in progress, and its attainment extremely difficult.

SUBMARINE LOSSES

Chronological

North Sea N.—North of 58°; North Sea—58° to 53°; North Sea S.—South of 53°. Channel E.—East of 0°; Channel—0° to 3° W.; Channel West—3° to 5° W.

1914	Aug. 9	U	15	North Sea N.
	Sept. 12	U	13	North Sea
	Nov. 23	U	18	North Sea N.
	Dec.	U	5	North Sea S.
	Dec.	U	11	North Sea S.
1915	Jan.	U	7	North Sea
	Jan.	U	31	Unknown
	Mar. 4	U	8	Dover Area
	Mar. 10	U	12	North Sea
(10)	Mar. 18	U	29	North Sea
	June 5	U	14	North Sea
	June 23	U	40	North Sea
	June (ca.)	U	37	North Sea
	July 2	UC	2	North Sea S.
	July 20	U	23	North Sea N.
	July 24	U	36	Scotland NW.
	Aug. 11	UB	4	North Sea S.

	Aug. 19	U	27	Irish Chan. Appr.
	Aug. (ca.)	UB	1	Medit.
(20)	Aug.	U	26	Baltic
	Sept. 15	U	6	North Sea N.
	Sept. 24	U	41	Chan. Approach
	Oct. 6 (ca.)	UC	9	North Sea S.
	Nov. 4	UC	8	North Sea
1916	Mar. 17	UC	12	Medit. E.
	Mar. 22	U	68	Ireland SW.
	Mar. (ca.)	UB	13	Unknown
	Apr. 5	UB	26	Channel
	Apr. 23	UC	3	North Sea S.
(30)	Apr. 24	UB	3	North Sea S.
	Apr. 27	UC	5	North Sea S.
	May 27	U	74	North Sea
	May (ca.)	UB	15	Medit.
	May (or June)	U	10	North Sea S.
	July 6	UC	10	North Sea S.
	July 7	U	77	North Sea
	July 14	U	51	North Sea
	July 30	UB	44	Medit. E.
	Aug. 21	UC	7	North Sea S.
(40)	Oct. 30	UB	45	Black Sea
	Oct.	UB	7	Black Sea
	Nov. 2	U	56	Arctic
	Nov. 4	U	20	North Sea, Jutland
	Nov. 30	UB	19	Channel
	Nov.	UC	15	Black Sea
	Nov. (ca.)	UC	13	Medit.
	Dec. 4	UC	19	North Sea S.
	Dec. 6	UB	29	Channel Approach
	Dec. 16	UB	46	Dardanelles
1917	Jan. 14	UB	37	Channel
(51)	Jan. 26	U	76	Arctic
	Feb. 8	UC	39	North Sea
	Feb. 8	UC	46	North Sea S.
	Feb. 17	U	83	Ireland SW.
	Feb. 23	UC	32	North Sea
	Mar. 10	UC	43	North Sea N.
	Mar. 12	UC	18	North Sea
	Mar. 12	U	85	Channel W.
	Mar. 13	UB	6	Dutch Coast (Interned)
(60)	Apr. 5	UC	68	North Sea S.
	Apr. 19	UC	30	North Sea

	Date	Boat	Location
	May 1	U 81	Atlantic
	May 9	UC 26	North Sea S.
	May 14	U 59	North Sea
	May 17	UB 39	Channel
	May 20	UC 36	North Sea S.
	May 24	UC 24	Medit. E.
	June 7	UC 29	Ireland SW.
	June 12	UC 66	Channel W.
(70)	June 20	U 99	Ireland W.
	June	UB 36	Unknown
	July 12	U 69	North Sea N.
	July 24	UC 1	North Sea S.
	July 26	UC 61	Dover Area
	July 29	UB 23	Channel W. (then interned, Coruña)
	July 29	UB 27	North Sea S.
	July 29	UB 20	North Sea S.
	Aug. 4	UC 44	Ireland S. (Waterford)
	Aug. 12	U 44	North Sea N.
(80)	Aug. 18	UB 32	Channel
	Aug. 21	UC 41	North Sea (Tay)
	Sept. 2	U 28	Arctic
	Sept. 10	UC 42	Ireland S.
	Sept. 11	U 49	Atlantic
	Sept. 12	U 45	Ireland N.
	Sept. 17	U 88	Atlantic
	Sept. 22	UC 72	North Sea S.
	Sept. 26	UC 33	Irish Channel
	Sept. 27	UC 21	North Sea S.
(90)	Sept. 28	UC 6	North Sea S.
	Sept. 29	UC 55	North Sea N. (Lerwick)
	Oct. 1–11	U 50	North Sea
	Oct. 1–11	U 66	North Sea
	Oct. 5	UB 41	North Sea
	Oct. 5–9	U 106	North Sea
	Oct. 19	UC 79	North Sea S.
	Oct. 23	UC 16	Channel
	Oct. (ca.)	UC 62	North Sea
	Oct. (ca.)	UC 14	North Sea S.
(100)	Nov. 1	UC 63	North Sea S.
	Nov. 3	UC 65	Channel
	Nov. 13	UC 51	North Sea S.
	Nov. 17	U 58	Ireland S.
	Nov. 17	UB 18	Channel
	Nov. 18	UC 47	North Sea
	Nov. 19–22	UC 57	Baltic

	Date	Boat	Location
	Nov. 24	U 48	Dover Area
	Nov. 29	UB 61	North Sea S.
	Dec. 2	UB 81	Channel
(110)	Dec. 6	UC 69	Channel
	Dec. 10	UB 75	North Sea
	Dec. 13	U 75	North Sea
	Dec. 14	UC 38	Medit. E.
	Dec. 19	UB 56	Dover Area
	Dec. 25	U 87	Irish Channel
1918	Jan. 7	U 93	Channel Approach
	Jan. 8	UB 69	Medit. W.
	Jan. 18	UB 66	Medit. W.
	Jan. 19	UB 22	North Sea
(120)	Jan. 26	U 84	Irish Channel
	Jan. 26	UB 35	Dover Area
	Jan. 26	U 109	Dover Area
	Jan. 28	UB 63	North Sea N.
	Jan. (ca.)	U 95	Unknown
	Feb. 4	UC 50	Dover Area
	Feb. 8	UB 38	Dover Area
	Feb. 12	U 89	Ireland N.
	Feb. 25	UB 17	Channel
	Mar. 10	UB 58	Dover Area
(130)	Mar. 11	UB 54	North Sea
	Mar. 15	U 110	Ireland N.
	Mar. 23	UC 48	Interned, Ferrol
	Mar. 26	U 61	Irish Channel
	Apr. 11	UB 33	Dover Area
	Apr. 17	UB 82	Ireland N.
	Apr. 21	UB 71	Medit. W.
	Apr. 22	UB 55	Dover Area
	Apr. 25	U 104	Irish Channel
	Apr. 30	UB 85	Irish Channel
(140)	May 2	UB 31	Dover Area
	May 2	UC 78	Dover Area
	May 8	UB 70	Medit. W.
	May 8	U 32	Medit. W.
	May 9	UB 78	Channel
	May 10	UB 16	North Sea S.
	May 11	U 154	Atlantic
	May 12	U 103	Channel W.
	May 12	UB 72	Channel
	May 16	UC 35	Medit. W.
(150)	May 18	U 39	Interned, Cartagena
	May 23	UB 52	Medit. E.

	Date	Boat	Location
	May 24	UC 56	Interned, Santander
	May 26	UB 74	Channel
	Mar 31	UC 75	North Sea
	May 31	UC 49	North Sea
	May (ca.)	UB119	Unknown
	June 17	U 64	Medit. W.
	June 20	UC 64	Dover Area
	June 26	UC 11	North Sea S.
(160)	July 10	UC 77	Dover Area
	July 10	UB 65	Ireland SW.
	July 19	UB110	North Sea
	July 20	UB124	Ireland N.
	July 27	UB107	North Sea S.
	July (ca.)	UB108	Unknown
	Aug. 3	UB 53	Medit. E.
	Aug. 13	UB 30	North Sea
	Aug. 14	UB 57	North Sea S.
	Aug. 28	UC 70	North Sea
(170)	Aug. 29	UB109	Dover Area
	Aug. (ca.)	UB 12	North Sea S.
	Sept. 9	U 92	North Sea N.
	Sept. 10	UB 83	North Sea N.
	Sept. 16	UB103	Dover Area
	Sept. 19	UB104	North Sea N.
	Sept. 25	U 156	North Sea N.
	Sept. 29	UB115	North Sea N.
	Sept.	U 102	prob. North Sea N.
	Sept.	UB113	prob. North Sea
(180)	Sept.	UB127	prob. North Sea N.
	Oct. 4	UB 68	Medit. E.
	Oct. 16	UB 90	North Sea
	Oct. 19	UB123	North Sea N.
	Oct. 28	U 78	North Sea
	Oct. 28	UB116	North Sea N.
	Oct.	*U 47	Medit.
	Oct.	*U 65	Medit.
	Oct.	*U 72	Medit.
	Oct.	*U 73	Medit.
(190)	Oct.	*UB 10	North Sea S.
	Oct.	*UB 40	North Sea S.
	Oct.	*UB 48	Medit.
	Oct.	*UB 59	North Sea S.
	Oct.	*UB129	Medit.
	Oct.	*UC 4	North Sea S.
	Oct.	*UC 25	Medit.
	Oct.	*UC 34	Medit.

	Oct.		*UC	53	Medit.
	Oct.		*UC	54	Medit.
(200)	Nov.	9	U	34	Medit. W.

Losses after signing of Armistice

	Nov. 11	U	157	Interned, Norway
	Nov. 21	U	97	North Sea
	Nov. 21	UC	74	Interned, Barcelona

* Destroyed by the Germans on evacuation of Flanders and the Adriatic.

LIST OF GERMAN SUBMARINES SUNK

Commander's Name	Rank	Name of Sub.	Place	Date of Sinking
Albrecht, Kurt	Dead	K-1		
Albrecht, Werner	"	O-L	UC-53	
Amberger, Gustav	P. W.	K-L	UB-58	50:58N 01:14E	Mar. 10, 1918
Amberger, Wilhelm	Dead	O-L	UB-108	
Arnold, Alfred	P. W.	O-L		
Bachmann, Gunther	Dead	O-L	UB-38	50:56N 01:25W	Feb. 8, 1918
Barten, Wilhelm	"	O-L		
Bauck, W.	"	K-L	U-89		Feb. 1918
Bauer, Casar	"	K-L		
Bender, Waldemar	Escaped, returned to Germany	K-L	U-69	North Sea (N)	July 12, 1917
Berekhelm, Egewolf Freiherr von	Dead	K-L		
Berger, Gerardt	"	K-L	U-50	Near German Coast	Oct. 1917
Bermis, Kurt	"	K-L	U-104	51:59W 06:26W	April 26, 1918
Branchied, Albert	"	O-L	UB-17	Channel	Feb. 25, 1918
Braun, Charles	"	O-L		
Brever, Herbert	P. W.	O-L		
Buck, Gustav	Dead	K-L		
Degetau, Hans	"	O-L	U-68		Mar. 22,
Dieckmann, Victor	"	K-L	U-62	
Ditfurth, Benno von	"	O-L	UB-32	North Sea	Sept. 17,
Edling, Karl	"	K-L	U-48	Goodwins	Nov. 24, 1917
Ehrentraut, Otto	"	O-L	UC-39	54:03N 00:02	Feb. 8, 1918
Eltester, Max	"	K-L		
Feddersen, Adolf	L-	UC-14		
Fircks, Wilhelm Frieherr von	Dead	K-L		
Fischer, Karl-Hanno	"	L-		
Frohner, Eherhardt	"	L-		
Furbringer, Gerhardt	P. W.	K-L		
Furbringer, Werner	P. W.	K-L	UB-110	
Galster, Hans	Dead	O-L	UC-51		Dec. 1917
Gebeschus, Rudolf	"	K-L	UB-63	56:17 02:25W	Jan. 28, 1918
Gercke, Herman	"	K-L	U-154	In Atlantic Azores	May 11, 1918

149

Commander's Name		Rank	Name of Sub.	Place	Date of Sinking
Gerlach, Helmut	"	K-L	U-93	49:59 05:12W	Jan. 7, 1918
Gerth, George	P. W.	K-L	UC-61	Wissant Shoal near Gris Nez	July 26, 1917
Glimpf, Herman	Dead	O-L	UB-20	North Hinder	July 29, 1917
Graeff, Ernst	P. W.	K-L			
Gregor, Fritz	Dead	O-L	UB-33	Channel	April 14, 1918
Gross, Karl	"	O-L	UC-2	Off Yarmouth	July 2, 1915
Gunther, Paul	"	O-L	UB-37	50:07N 01:47W	Jan. 14, 1917
Guntzel, Ludwig	"	K-L			
Gunzel, Erich	"	K-L	U-75		Dec. 17,
Haag, George	"	L-	UB-13		Mar. 1916
Hansen, Klaus	"	K-L			
Hartman, Richard	"	K-L	U-49	46:17N 14:42W	Sept. 11, 1917
Hecht, Erich	"	O-L	UB-54	Channel	Mar. 11, 1918
Heinke, Curt	"	O-L			
Heller, Bruno	"	O-L			
Hennig, Heinrich von	P. W.	K-L			
Heydebreck, Karsten V.	Dead	O-L	UC-63	51-23N 02-00E	Nov. 1, 1917
Hirzel, Alfred	"	O-L			
Hoppe, Bruno	"	K-L			
Hufnagel, Hans	"	K-L	U-106	North Sea	Oct. 10, 1917
Kesserlingk, Harold V.	"	O-L	UB-36	North Sea	June, 1917
Kiel, Wilhelm	"	O-L	UC-18	54:38N 00-55N	Mar. 12, 1917
Kiesewetter, Wilhelm	Interned	K-L	UC-56	Santander	May 26, 1918
Klatt, Alfred	Dead	O-L	UC-38	Medit. 38:32N 20:34E	Dec. 14, 1917
Kolbe, Walther	"	O-L	UC-103	40 miles South of Lizard Point	May 11, 1918
Konig, Gerog	"	K-L			
Korsch, Hans Paul	"	O-L	UC-35	Sardinia	May 16, 1918
Kratzsch	"	K-L			
Krech, Gunther	P. W.	K-L	UB-85	N. Channel	April 30, 1918
Kreysern, Gunther	Dead	O-L	UC-3	52:24N 02:24E	April 23, 1916
Kroll, Karl	"	K-K	U-110	55:49N 08:00W	Mar. 15, 1918
Kustner, Heinrich	"	O-L	UB-39	50:05N 01:25W	May 17, 1917
Lafrenze, Claus P.	P. W.	K-L	UC-65	50:28N 00:17E	Nov. 3, 1917
Launburg, Otto	P. W.	O-L	UB-52	Adriatic	May 23, 1918
Lammer, Johannes	Dead	K-L			
Lepsius, Rienhald	"	O-L			
Lilienstern, Ruhler	"	O-L	UC-55	60:00N 01:00W	Sept. 29, 1917
Lorenze, Hellmuth	Interned	O-L	UC-48	50:22N 01:47W	Mar. 23, 1918
Lorenze, Herman	Dead	K-L			
Lowe, Werner	"	O-L	UB-58	50:58N 01:14E	Mar. 10, 1918
Luhe, Vicco von der	P. W.	O-L	UB-16	North Sea	May 10, 1918
Menzel, Bernhard	Dead	O-L			
Metz, Artur	"	O-L			
Metzger, Heinrich	Interned	K-L	U-39	Carthagena	May 18, 1918
Mey, Karl	Dead	O-L			
Mildenstein, Christian	"	O-L	UC-1		July, 1917
Moecke, Fritz	"	O-L			
Mohrbutter, Urich	P. W.	O-L			
Moraht Robert	P. W.	K-L	U-64	Bizerta, Medit.	June 21, 1918
Muhlan, Helmut	P. W.	K-L			
Muhle, Gerhardt	Dead	K-L			

Commander's Name	Rank	Name of Sub.	Place	Date of Sinking
Muller, Hans Albrecht "	O–L			
Neumann, Friedrich P. W.	O–L	UB–5		
Niemer, Hans Interned	O–L	UB–23		July 26, 1917
Niemeyer, Georg Dead	O–L			
Nitzsche, Alfred "	O–L			
Noodt, Erich P. W.	O–L			
Petz, Willy Dead	K–L	U–85	49:52N 03:20W	Mar. 12, 1917
Platsch, Erich "	O–L			
Pohle, Richard "	K–L			
Prinz, Athalwin "	K–L			
Pustkuchen, Herbert "	O–L	UC–66	49:56N 05:10W	June 12, 1917
Reichenback, Gottfried "	O–L	UC–6	51:37N 02:51E	Sept. 28, 1917
Reimarus, Georg "	O–L	UC–21	51:30N 01:34E	Sept. 20, 1917
Remy, Johannes "	K–L			
Roehr, Walter "	K–L	U–84	55–53N 05:44W	Jan. 25, 1918
Rosenow, Ernest "	K–L	UC–29	51:47N 11:40W	June 7, 1917
Rumpel, Walther "	K–L			
Rucker, Claus "	K–L	U–103	51:03N 01–38E	Jan. 26, 1918
Saltzwedel, Rudolf "	O–L	UB–81	30:27N 00:53	Dec. 2, 1917
Sebelin, Erwin "	K–L			
Seuffer, Rudolf "	K–L	UC–50	50:47N 00:59E	Feb. 4, 1918
Schmettow, Graf von "	K–L	UC–26	51:3N 1:40E	May 9, 1917
Schmidt, Georg "				
Schmidt, Siegfried "	O–L	U–45	55–48N 7:30W	Sept. 12, 1917
Schmidt, Walther G. Interned	O–L	UC–56	Santander	May 5, 1918
Schmitz, Max Dead	O–L	UC–62		
Schmitz, Walther P. W.	O–L	UC–75	Off Tyne	May 31, 1918
Schneider, Rudolf Dead	K–L	U–87	52:56N 05:07W	Dec. 27, 1917
Schultz, Theodor "	O–L	UB–61		Dec. 1917
Schurmann, Paul "	O–L	UC–4		Oct. 15, 1917
Schwartz, Ferdinand "	O–L	UB–64		
Schweinitz und Krain				
Graf von "	K–L			
Schwieger "	K–L	U–88	49:42N 13:18W	Sept. 14, 1917
Sittenfield, Erich "	K–L	U–45	55–48N 7:30W	Sept. 12, 1917
Smith, Wilhelm P. W.	O–L			
Soergel, Hans Dead	O–L			
Sprenger P. W.	K–L	UC–34		
Steckelberg, Oscar Interned	O–L	UB–6	Dutch Coast	Mar. 13, 1917
Stein Zu Lausnitz				
Freiherr von Dead	O–L	UB–27	52:47N 02:24E	July 29, 1917
Steindoff, Ernest "	O–L	UB–74	5 miles S. Port- land Bill	May 26, 1918
Stenzler, Heinrich "	O–L	UB–78	Off Cherbourg	May 9, 1918
Stosberg, Arthur P. W.	O–L	UB–78		
Stoss, Alfred P. W.	K–L			
Stoter, Karl Dead	O–L	UB–35	51:03N 01:38E	Jan. 26, 1918
Stuhr, Fritz "	K–L	U–10	51:26N 20:50E	May 19, 1916
Suchodoletz, Ferdi-				
nand V. "	K–L			
Tebbenjohannes, Kurt P. W.	K–L	UC–44	52:07N 6:59W	Aug. 4, 1917
Trager, Friedrich Dead	O–L	UB–72	26 miles SSW Portland Bill	May 12, 1918
Utke, Kurt P. W.	O–L	UC–11	E. Harwich	June 26, 1918

Commander's Name	Rank	Name of Sub.	Place	Date of Sinking
Valentiner, Hans	Dead	O-L	U-156	
			or U-157 50:58N 01:28E	Dec. 1917
Voigt, Ernest	"	O-L	UC-72 Stranded in	
			Dover Sept. or Oct.	1917
Wachendorff, Seigfried	"	O-L		
Wacker, Karl	"	O-L	UB-22	Jan. 1918
Wagenfuhr, Paul	"	O-L	U-44 58-51N 4-40E	Aug. 12, 1917
Walther, Franz	"	O-L	UB-75	
Weddigan, Otto	"	K-L		
Wegener, Bernhard	"	K-L		
Weisbach, Erwin	"	K-L	U-32 Mediterranean	May 1, 1918
Weisbach, Raimund	P. W.	K-L	U-81 51N 13W	May 1, 1917
Wendlandt, Hans H.	P. W.	O-L	UC-38 Medit. 38:32N	Dec. 14, 1917
			20:34E	
Wenninger, Ralph	P. W.	K-L	UB-55 Channel E.	April 22, 1918
Wigankow, Gunther	Dead	O-L		
Wilcke, Erich	"	K-L		
Wilhelms, Ernest	"	K-L		
Willich, Kurt	"	K-L	UC-24 Off Cattaro	May 24, 1917
Wutsdorff, Hans Osker	"	K-L		
Zerboni, di Sposetti Werner von	"	K-L	UC-16	Oct. 1917

A Short Biography of Admiral Sims

By Cora W. Rowell

There were three boys in the Sims family, and one day their father announced that he had just received an appointment to Annapolis for one of his sons. It had to be decided immediately which one should go. Two of the boys thought that they would not care for the navy, and the choice fell upon William.

William was seventeen at the time, and until then probably the thought of a naval career had not entered his mind. He had been born at Port Hope in Ontario in 1858, but had lived the most of his life on a farm in western Pennsylvania.

The opportunity which had come so unexpectedly found him quite unprepared. He had never been a student. In fact, "his greater pleasure was not to learn," and in school he was counted a slow and rather careless pupil.

The competitive examinations for Annapolis in those days comprised mostly grammar school subjects, but they were difficult, and the passing mark was high. William took them and failed. Then there came an awakening.

It was not customary to give candidates who failed a second chance, but William Sims begged so hard that the examiners finally consented. And they gave him a month in which to prepare.

At the end of the month, he went up again for his examinations, and this time he passed. He had worked "terrifically."

He had now four years of hard study ahead of him, and he soon discovered that his scholarship no longer concerned himself alone but reflected on the standing of his company. If he made a poor recitation or "busted cold," in the language of the cadets, his classmates turned their thumbs down. He was slated for disapproval. If his marks were unsatisfactory, he was put on the "tree," the published list of those who are poor in scholarship, and other members of the company made it very uncomfortable for him. On the other hand, if he made an average of eighty-five *per cent* throughout the year, he was entitled to wear a gold star on the collar of his uniform the next year and become a popular man with his mates.

There were two studies that William Sims particularly disliked, French and mathematics. Since these were especially necessary for a naval officer, he made up his mind to overcome his dislike for them. He succeeded so well that, after his graduation, he asked for a year's leave of absence in order that he might go to Paris to complete his study of French. Today he speaks French quite as well as English.

He learned other things that first year not included in the curriculum. His company saw that his scholarship was high, but upper-class men looked after his table manners. "Boat your oars," a senior would call out to the embarrassed freshman when knife and fork rested against his plate, or "Rig in your boom," if his elbows stuck out.

Regulations met him at every turn. Most of them had to do with his conduct in class or at drill, but a few, it seemed, were designed to govern even his leisure time. He must always appear with his shoes blackened and his uniform carefully brushed, and everything in his room must be in order. When off duty, however, he was on his honour. A midshipman's word was never questioned. Any misconduct was his own affair, but there was always the honour of the class to be upheld, and the class did not deal leniently with offenders.

After graduating from the Academy, a midshipman was required to spend two years at sea before he could become an officer of the navy. William Sims found that the life at sea admitted of considerable improvement. With twenty-one others he occupied the forecastle of an old sailing ship. The quarters were small and the ventilation was bad. On hot nights the men could hardly breathe. Sims complained to the commanding officer.

"As human beings," he said, "we are entitled to so many cubic feet of air."

"You don't say!" replied the captain. "Get to your quarters and remember, young man, that there ain't anything human about a midshipman."

Sims then wrote to the navy department. When no reply came to his letter, he wrote again. Meanwhile he had investigated the amount of air space in barns and found that midshipmen were allowed less than pigs and cattle. Though it was considered almost an act of effrontery on the part of a midshipman, he sent his figures in to Washington.

The improvement of midshipmen's quarters which finally resulted was the first of many reforms Sims was to bring about.

For the next eighteen years, however, not much was heard of him except that he was doing his work well. A part of that time he was instructor on the school ships Saratoga and Philadelphia. Two years he spent in China and the far East. Promotion in the navy in times of peace is extremely slow, and at forty Sims was still a lieutenant.

When the Spanish-American War came, in 1898, he was naval *attaché* to the American Embassy at Paris. Probably it was his knowledge of French that had gained him the appointment.

There is a story that, in the beginning of the war. Lieutenant Sims was ordered to Liverpool to hurry the shipment of a cargo of ammunition much needed by our troops in Cuba. About the time the order was ready, word came that the Spanish fleet had sailed for America, and the Liverpool firm refused to let the loaded ship start unless it was insured against loss. Time was too valuable to wait for the government to act, and Lieutenant Sims pledged himself personally to be responsible for any loss if the ship would only sail before sunset. At the time he did not consider how long it would take him to pay the bill, but afterwards he was amazed when he remembered that the value of the cargo was a million dollars.

His work in Paris and Petrograd, where he also served as naval *attaché*, gave him the opportunity to see what other navies were doing, and he woke up to the fact that the American Navy was very inferior to those of European nations. We had beautiful ships, trim, clean, and white, but they were not fighting ships. Again, Sims reported his observations to the navy department. His letters were filed away and nothing came of them.

In 1900 he was again transferred to the China station. He reported for duty on the U. S. S. *Kentucky*, which had put in at Gibraltar on its way to the Orient. The *Kentucky* was a ship of the type to which Sims had objected. Though her captain thought she was the pride of the navy, the junior officer, "with two fingers on the typewriter," says Lieutenant Reuterdahl, "pointed out that she was no ship at all."

"We should have shed tears when we launched her," he argued, "instead of sprinkling her with champagne." The report which went to Washington found its way into a pigeon hole marked "Lieutenant Sims."

Out in China Sims met a British naval officer named Captain Percy Scott, who was interested in new methods, and the two officers became good friends.

One day Captain Scott told Sims that he had invented a device for improving the marksmanship of his gunners. It was generally conceded at the time that the marksmanship in all navies was poor, for ammunition was too expensive to permit of gun practice every day. Captain Scott's device was simple and inexpensive. To the barrel of a big gun was attached a tube, which fired a bullet at a small target set up at close range. If the small target was hit, the gun was accurately aimed to hit the large target miles away.

Sims was much impressed with this scheme and made use of it on a number of the guns of the *Kentucky*. At the next target practice the marksmanship of his crews surpassed that of all the other crews in the Asiatic fleet. This convinced him that the scheme was a practical one, and he wrote at once to Washington, sending a full report of his experiment and urging that Captain Scott's system be adopted by the American Navy.

Months passed and no reply came. Sims knew as well as anyone that the destination of all his letters was either a pigeon hole or a waste basket, but he kept on writing. His thought then, as it had been from the first, was to improve the service. His reports, however, had not resulted in any change of system, for an inefficient navy reflected on the navy department, and the department did not want a lieutenant out in China to show up its faults.

Nevertheless, the letters continued to come, and finally one reached President Roosevelt himself.

Meanwhile information had come from other sources that the navy was not very efficient. In the Spanish War, so recently ended, the records of our fleet showed that, out of every hundred shots fired on the Cuban coast, only four had reached the mark.

Therefore, when President Roosevelt received Lieutenant Sims's letter, he determined to find out for himself whether the marksmanship in the navy was really as bad as had been reported. If it was, something should be done about it, but if it was not. Lieutenant Sims, who had come very near to criticizing his superior officers, ought to lose his rank. Five of the best battleships of the Atlantic fleet were ordered out, and for five hours they steamed back and forth firing at a target larger than the one used regularly for gun practice. An examination of the mark at the end of that time showed that only three hits had been made.

When President Roosevelt heard this, he immediately recalled

Lieutenant Sims from China and put him in charge of the navy's target practice.

The building of a more effective navy was to be Sims's work. The methods which he introduced were then little known; today they would be termed the methods of scientific management. With a stop watch he timed and coordinated the movements of a crew so that not a moment was wasted in the firing of a gun. In this way he reduced the firing time from five minutes to thirty seconds. He told the bluejackets that higher ratings and extra pay would be given to the men who made the best records, and soon there was great rivalry among crews. A good gun pointer became the most popular man aboard ship. Then it was ship against ship and squadron against squadron for the honour of flying the pennant of the winner.

A record to compare with that of our fleet during the Spanish War is that of the *South Carolina*, a few years after Sims's methods had been introduced. Firing twelve-inch guns, one of the *Carolina's* crews recorded sixteen hits out of sixteen shots in four minutes thirty-one seconds. This was battle practice; our navy had learned to shoot.

Another of Sims's reforms was to create a better spirit between officers and men. In the old days an officer would have said, in the words of Sims's first captain, that there was nothing human about a bluejacket. An officer's duty was to work his men as long and as hard as he could. With this way of thinking Sims radically disagreed. He believed that a friendly feeling between officers and men was necessary to the making of a better navy.

"The happy ship," he said, "is almost invariably the efficient ship," and he began another one of his investigations. The many ways he found of adding to the comforts of the men won their loyalty at once.

On board the superdreadnought *Nevada*, which Sims commanded just before the European war, the bluejackets wanted some way of showing their affection for Captain Sims and decided to make some doormats for his cabin. Knowing his motto to be "Cheer up and get busy," they wove the first part of it into the mats, so that everyone stepping across the threshold was invited to "cheer up." Then in the cabin port holes they arranged electric lights that threw out on the decks the words, "Get busy." This was the relationship between officer and men that Sims worked constantly to bring about. It is said that in ten years his reforms have revolutionized the navy's spirit.

Some twenty years ago the question of larger ships was being considered by naval experts all over the world. The biggest ship of the day was the battleship, which carried both large and small guns. In 1903 Lieutenant Homer C. Poundstone of the American Navy invented a great heavy armoured, high-speed ship with all big guns. Sims was much interested in this new type of craft and, with Lieutenant Poundstone, worked out all the details of the plan. Both officers believed it to be the fighting ship of the future. They named it the U. S. S. *Scared-o-Nothing*. Two years later, there appeared in the Royal Navy an all-big-gun ship, the first of the kind to be built. It was called the *Dreadnought*.

From the time Sims first heard of Lieutenant Poundstone's big ship, he had tried repeatedly to have the plans accepted by the navy department, but it was not until Great Britain and Italy actually began to build dreadnoughts that the department finally consented. Plans for the *Michigan* and the *South Carolina*, which had been ordered as battleships, were then changed and these became our first dreadnoughts.

One other achievement of Sims's was to prove of great value in the European war. This was his work with the destroyers. In 1911, when Captain Sims was a man of fifty-three, he entered the Naval War College at Newport, Rhode Island, and worked there as an ordinary student for two years, chiefly upon the problems of destroyers.

Destroyers were comparatively new ships in the navy and it was not very clear what their function in battle was to be, whether they should keep to the work for which they were originally built, destroying torpedo boats, or whether they should be used in attack against the giant battleships. If they were to be used in attack, their movements must be regulated and timed.

When Sims left the War College, he was given command of the Torpedo Flotilla of the Atlantic fleet, which afforded him the opportunity of trying out in a practical way the problems over which he had worked. He converted the destroyer flotilla from a mere collection of ships into a coordinated fighting machine, and it was this work which enabled us to take our place in the fighting line just five weeks after war was declared with Germany.

Sims was President of the Naval War College when war came. Shortly afterwards he was promoted to the rank of vice-admiral, and since the war has ended, he has been made an admiral, which is the highest rank in the navy.

Before war was actually declared, he was sent to London to confer with the British Admiralty. He has himself told the story of his departure.

While I was President of the Naval War College at Newport, I was ordered to report without delay to the Secretary of the Navy at Washington. I was not notified of the nature of the business to be discussed. When I arrived, I was received in secret conference with Secretary Daniels and Admiral Benson, chief of naval operations.

I was told that it looked as though we should go to war with Germany. They then explained to me that I was to go at once to see the people on the other side and reach an understanding as to how the United States could best cooperate with the Allied sea force in operation against Germany.

They told me that one *aide* would be allowed me and that his identity must not be known until it might be decided to reveal it on his arrival on the other side.

I chose Commander J. V. Babcock, who was my *aide* at Newport. We both put on civilian clothes, dropped our names, and assumed others more suitable to the occasion. Babcock and I chose 'Richardson' and 'Robertson' as near as I can recall. We sailed from New York on March 31, 1917, on the steamship *New York*. No one on the steamer recognised us, and we passed the trip as ordinary voyagers.

We received the news of the declaration of war by the ship's wireless on April 6th, but it did not disturb us. We reached Liverpool on April 9th in a thick fog. Entering the harbour, the *New York* struck a mine, which blew a hole in one of her forward compartments.

At Liverpool we went ashore like anyone else. A special train was waiting at the landing stage, however, with Admiral Hope of the British Admiralty. It waited there until we got aboard, then pulled out for London.

We arrived at London April 10th, still wearing civilian clothes. We went at once to the Admiralty offices, where we had a conference with Admiral Jellicoe.

On April 13th, at a luncheon in London, the United States Ambassador made a formal announcement that I had arrived in the country. After that I went about in uniform.

The first of our ships to reach the fighting zone were the destroyers. From their camouflage they were known as "Sims's circus." They were barred, striped, and daubed in all colours. Breaking the outline renders a ship less visible to the enemy and often makes it difficult to tell in which direction it is moving.

The destroyers had sailed, prepared in every detail for war, yet not even the commander knew that the flotilla was bound for Europe. The instructions were to "proceed to a point fifty miles east of Cape Cod and there to open sealed orders."

The Germans, however, had learned of the sailing of the flotilla, knew of its destination and the day of its arrival, and, the night before it was to reach Queenstown, Ireland, had planted a field of mines at the entrance to the harbour. In spite of this effort on the part of the enemy, our destroyers slipped into port safely, the Stars and Stripes flying from their masts, "their funnels white with salt spray."

On shore a crowd had gathered to greet them and, from the time they were first sighted, filing in a long line into the harbour, cheer after cheer went up, until they finally dropped anchor and the officers came ashore.

It was a simple greeting of a few hundred people, quite different from the one Queenstown had planned. Military bands and a celebration to last several days had been ordered, but at the last moment Admiral Sims arrived and asked that all preparations be stopped. Our destroyers were not coming for pleasure, he said, but to fight.

Nevertheless, the British commander who greeted our flotilla was hardly prepared for the senior officer's answer to his question, "When will you be ready for service?"

"We can start at once, sir," the American commander replied. It was expected that the destroyers would need time to prepare for war service.

"We made preparations on the way over," the American officer continued. "That is why we are ready." And within an hour after their arrival at Queenstown the destroyers were on their way to the fighting zone.

At this time, as Admiral Sims has since said, the Germans were winning the war. Every month their submarines destroyed between 700,000 and 800,000 tons of Allied shipping. The American Navy adopted new methods of combating submarines. At first, they were only experiments, but they proved so successful that the shipping losses rapidly decreased from that time on. The principal methods used were three: first, the convoy system, which was Admiral Sims's own idea; second, the depth bomb; and third, the listening device for detecting submarines. The last two were American inventions, sent over by the American Board of Inventions.

To fight submarines was especially the work of the destroyers. They are slender, trim looking ships, some three hundred feet long, with a breadth of only thirty feet. Steaming at high speed, a destroyer darts upon a submarine, endeavouring to ram it before it can submerge. Failing to do this, it then wheels in circles or in zigzag lines and drops its depth bombs. The bombs explode eighty feet below the sea's surface, destroying everything within one hundred fifty yards. They have accounted for more submarines than any other single device.

A naval officer on board one of our first transports tells what happened during a submarine attack when a destroyer came to the rescue, (*Our Navy in the War*, Lawrence Perry.)

Like a striking rattlesnake, it darted between a couple of transports. Her nose was so deep in the sea as to be almost buried, while a great wave at the stern threw a shower of spray on the soldiers massed at the transport's bow. That destroyer ran right along the line of bubbles like a hound following a trail, and when it came to the spot where the commander estimated the submarine must be lurking he released a depth bomb. A column of smoke and foam rose fifty feet in the air, and the destroyer herself rose half out of the water under the shock of the explosion. On the water were seen oil and fragments of wood and steel.

Convoy work was exacting, patrol duty hardly less so. In seas strewn with wreckage, where any stick resembled a periscope, a patrol ship had to be on the alert constantly. A destroyer on patrol sometimes covered six or seven thousand miles a month, and its patrol beat might be anywhere from the Mediterranean to the North Sea.

But, whatever the dangers and hardships, hunting submarines was "the greatest game in the world," and both officers and men counted themselves lucky to be with the destroyers. A song went round among the crews that ran like this:

Talk about your battleships, cruisers, scouts, and all;
Talk about your Fritzers who are waiting for a fall;
Talk about your Coast Guard, it's brave they have to be;
But Admiral Sims's flotilla is the terror of the sea."

The number of our destroyers in the beginning of the war was, however, too small to meet the needs of the patrol service, and soon

France sent in a call for more ships to guard her coasts. Until more destroyers could be built, the only available ships were those of the naval auxiliary, private yachts turned over to the navy for war service.

So frail did they appear for the task ahead of them that the navy men dubbed them the "Suicide Fleet." Their crews numbered a few enlisted men and one or two petty officers. The rest were chiefly college students. What they lacked in training they made up for in their eagerness to serve; when it came to fighting submarines, no destroyer fleet was going to get ahead of them.

Arriving at Brest one day, the Suicide Fleet found no end of work waiting for it. It had been sent for chiefly to convoy shipping along the French coast. This was the route to the Mediterranean and here the submarines were most active. Much of the convoying had to be done at night. With twenty to thirty merchant ships depending on it for safety, one of these yachts would feel its way in the darkness through the dangerous reefs and shoals of the Bay of Biscay, reaching some port only to take on coal and depart immediately. There was neither rest nor leisure for the crews as long as their boats held together.

In the chart room there was always a pile of radio messages. And too often there came a message which read like this, (*With the Fighting Fleets*, Ralph D. Paine):

From S. S.——, S. O. S. Am being torpedoed, thirty miles west of ——. Shot just missed by five hundred yards. Am being shelled. Hope to see you soon.

To which the yacht would reply:

Keep on that course. We are heading for you. Hold on! Help coming!

Perhaps the ship that was being shelled was one of a convoy in which case the other ships were obliged to steer a wild, zigzag course to escape a similar fate. Not infrequently they collided. If it were night, darkness added to the confusion. Unable to see the submarine, they would fire in the direction where they thought it might be. The answer was shells and more shells. Explosions told where a ship was struck, explosions and the cries of men calling for help as they floated about in the icy water.

Steaming up to a scene like this, the yacht would begin rescue work. Flashing on a searchlight, though to do so was to risk being torpedoed, she circled round and round, gathering in the men one

162

at a time. She did not get them all. Some drifted quickly out of sight; others went down before she could reach them. Most of those rescued made work for the ship's doctor. Generally, they were either wounded or frozen. Only now and then a man would clamber up the ship's side, grinning, and call out cheerfully, "Where do we go from here?"

The storms that battered them were some of the worst ever known in the east Atlantic. Heavy seas smashed, masts, life boats, and now and then the bow of a ship itself. Wind at sixty to a hundred miles an hour would roll them over until their funnels all but touched the water. Torpedoed in a sea like this, they were helpless; the waves would sweep the men overboard before they could reach their guns. Often it meant suicide for them to put to sea, yet they never failed to leave on schedule. Going down was only a part of the "great game."

So entirely was the attention of the Americans centred upon German submarines that for a time they forgot that we had submarines of our own. For months after the declaration of war nothing was heard of them. They worked quietly, patrolling our coasts, guarding our harbours. Then one day the Secretary of the Navy announced that a flotilla of American submarines had crossed the Atlantic. They had crossed in December of 1917 in severe winter storms which had carried them far out of their course and made their crossing a memorable achievement.

The captain of one of these submarines wrote, (*With the American Submarines*, Henry B. Beston, *Atlantic Monthly*, November, 1918):

On all the boats the lookout on the bridge had to be lashed in place, and every once in a while, a couple of tons of water would come tumbling over him.

You can imagine what it was like inside. To begin with, the oily air was none too sweet, because every time we opened a hatch, we shipped enough water to make the old hooker look like a start at a swimming tank; and then she was lurching so continuously and violently that to move six feet was an expedition. The men were wonderful, wonderful! Each man at his allotted task and—what's that English word?—carrying on. Our little cook couldn't do a thing with his stove, might as well have tried to cook on a miniature earthquake, but he saw that all of us had something to eat, doing his bit game as could be.

Since it was impossible to make any headway, we lay to for forty-eight hours. The deck began to go the second morning, some of the plates being ripped off. And blow—I never saw anything like it. The disk of the sea was just one great ragged mass of foam being hurled through space by a wind screaming past with the voice of a million express trains.

Perhaps you are wondering why we didn't submerge. We simply couldn't use up our electricity. It takes oil and running on the surface to create the electric power, and we had a long, long journey ahead. Then ice began to form on the superstructure, and we had to get out a crew to chop it off. It was something of a job; there wasn't much to hang on to, and the waves were still breaking over us. But we freed her of the danger and she went on.

After three weeks of this, when Admiral Sims was beginning to feel some anxiety about his submarines, they came into port one day, shipshape, with flags flying. They were to become a part of the submarine patrol, working in waters around the British Isles. Their work also was to hunt enemy submarines. By means of the listening device a German submarine could be detected miles away. Once an enemy boat was followed eighteen hours by an American submarine before it was caught.

"But aren't our submarines ever mistaken for German?" someone asked a submarine officer.

"Oh, yes," he answered in a matter-of-fact way.

To be mistaken for the enemy, to have torpedoes fired at you and depth bombs dropped on you, to run the risk of being rammed by one of your own destroyers—that was all a part of the business of the submarine patrol. There was even a grimmer side than this. That was to go scouting about under the sea and come unexpectedly upon the enemy. A British captain remarked:

Sometimes, nobody knows just what happens. Out there in the deep water, whatever happens, happens in a hurry.

And on the navy records there is entered against the number of the submarine which met the enemy simply the item, "Failed to report."

One day, some months after we entered the war, there arrived at an English port five strange looking battleships, with towers of latticed steel unlike anything in European Navies. An English writer says:

At sight of them, the grey, war-weary battle fleet of Britain burst into a roar of welcome such as had never before greeted a stranger within the gates, either in peace or war.

That same day Admiral Sims cabled the navy department in Washington:

Arrived as per schedule.

The American battleships had come to take part in the fighting, for it was expected that more naval battles would be fought before the end of the war. Since the Battle of Jutland, May 31, 1916, the German fleet had remained at home, yet every now and then there came a rumour that the enemy was out. On these occasions the British Fleet would leave its base and search the whole North Sea. Such an alarm was sounded soon after the arrival of our battleships. "Under way at three o'clock," was the order, and in the silence and darkness of early morning the whole fleet moved out. The place of honour was given to the American ships, which, operating as part of the British Fleet, now became known as the Sixth Battle Squadron. Steaming in line, just so many hundred yards apart, each battleship kept in its appointed place; following, came the cruisers, the destroyers, and the submarines.

Morning brought wind, rain, and fog. "No weather for a scrap unless it is a short and merry one," an officer remarked, and disappointment settled upon the Americans. It was due them to have just one "crack" at the Germans.

The high seas were making life most uncomfortable aboard ship, (*With the Fighting Fleets*, Ralph D. Paine):

Men moved with care lest they toboggan across the deck and break a leg. Water swashed in when the gun-ports rolled under, and barelegged bluejackets were baling the floors with buckets. It was damp, gloomy, and dismal below with the hatches battened, but the ships had bucked through heavier seas than this, and these hundreds of American sailors were salt-water philosophers.

Despite the weather the fleet still headed for the German coast. A stick appearing suddenly a few hundred yards to the starboard brought down a shell from the gunners. No risks could be taken in these waters, and the red flag, warning of submarines, was sent up the signal yard.

After twelve hours without sight of the enemy, the fleet reluctantly turned back. It was no use to go on in such weather. The next time, perhaps, there would be better luck.

The opportunity to engage the German fleet in battle, however, never came. The only time our battleships met the enemy was on the day when the German fleet surrendered, and the Sixth Battle Squadron, as part of the Grand Fleet, escorted it to May Island off the coast of Scotland.

It happened that on Christmas some of our battleships were in port. (*With the Fighting Fleets*, Ralph D. Paine.)

"Heard about it?" asked a sergeant of the marines.

"Well, there was Christmas trees and fake fireplaces all over the ships and socks hung up for dear old Santa Claus to slide down through the ventilator. And the admiral pulled off his favourite stunt, which was to invite a million or so poor kids aboard and give them a party. Counting noses, I suppose there was a thousand of them, to get it right. They were war orphans or their daddies were serving in France. We blew them off to a turkey dinner and a moving picture show and clothes and shoes and ten shillings, in cash, per kid, and what they couldn't eat without busting they carried home in paper bags. It was no trouble at all to raise funds. And was it worth it? Say, you forgot to be homesick.

"The kids sang Christmas songs and cheered the flag and the admiral and the crews and the navy. Then a gang of minstrels came over in boats from some British ships and serenaded us and we gave them a band concert and, when we turned in that night, it didn't seem such a bum Christmas after all."

When our navy had been at war a little more than a year it numbered a thousand ships. The trade routes for which it was responsible were not as many as Great Britain's, but our coast line was longer. From Puget Sound to San Diego Bay, from Maine to Panama, and on the shores of the Great Lakes, our patrols protected transports and shipping. Our dreadnoughts and battleships, with the exception of those in foreign service, formed a line of defence extending along the entire Atlantic coast and served also as training schools for war.

Submarine nets protected our harbours, mine sweepers worked continuously outside the harbour entrances to keep them free from mines, while scout boats and submarines watched for any sign of the enemy in American waters. All this was the "silent service" about which one heard little, but without which our fighting fleets could not have carried on.

Occasionally passers-by on the streets of London would turn to look at a tall straight man, wearing the blue uniform of the American Navy, and remark, "That's Admiral Sims." He was usually seen going or coming from one of two places, the British Admiralty or a mansion in Grosvenor Gardens, West London, over which floated the American flag. This latter place was Admiral Sims's office, the London headquarters of the American Navy.

It was through this office that all information reached Washington regarding the needs and organisation of our navy in the war zone. Methods and plans changed as the character of the war changed, and all instructions had to come from Admiral Sims.

From the moment he arrived in London he made it clear that the policy of the American Navy was not to be one of rivalry but of co-operation with our allies. If the British had methods that were better than ours, we should adopt British methods. The real object being to win the war, it did not matter by what methods the end was achieved.

It was the business of Admiral Sims's organisation, too, to watch the enemy, to know what German boats were on the seas and their approximate location. Reports reached the London office daily, and orders were flashed to ships from the North Sea to the Mediterranean.

In June of 1917 Admiral Sims was given command of the Allied fleets in Irish waters. It was the first honour of its kind that the Royal Navy had ever paid to a foreign naval officer. This work required that he spend a large part of his time at Queenstown, Ireland, and a fine old house, with beautiful lawns and gardens, situated on the heights above the town, was turned over to him.

His office at sea was on board the *Melville*, mother ship of a destroyer squadron, but he never remained very long in one place. One day he might be in London, the next in Paris, and on the third day at the naval base. Though he worked long hours, sometimes staying in his office until midnight, he was careful to keep in the best of health. He has always enjoyed his work above everything.

Some of his English friends have tried to interest him in hunting and fishing, but he is not a sportsman; he does not like to kill birds or animals. His idea of recreation is something quite different. In his spare moments he gets a great deal of fun from writing limericks and humorous verse.

An English correspondent writes:

One night when the American fleet was lying at anchor in

the Bay of Guaconabays, the officers assembled to discuss naval subjects. Sims was leaning on a table, busy with pen and paper. Officers thought that the admiral was occupied with an order or a dispatch. After an hour he handed each officer a limerick on the subject he had been discussing.

One other pleasure which Admiral Sims enjoys quite as much as his work is playing games of all sorts with his children. When he was President of the Naval War College, he used to ride a bicycle to school every morning with one of the children perched on the handlebars. Callers at his home have frequently found him sitting on the floor, entertaining the baby.

Outside of the navy, people have known very little about Admiral Sims. He prefers not to be known, and has asked reporters repeatedly not to mention his name in dispatches. Lieutenant Reuterdahl, writing of Admiral Sims, says that he has known him for seventeen years and has never been permitted to tell a story about him.

First and last his thought has been for the navy. Officers agree that Admiral Sims, more than any other person, has been responsible for making our navy efficient. The principles for which he has fought so persistently, however, include not only better methods of doing things, but improved conditions of work and a friendly relationship between officers and men. It is the recognition of the human quality in work which Admiral Sims believes makes for the highest type of efficiency.

LEONAUR

ALSO FROM LEONAUR
AVAILABLE IN SOFTCOVER OR HARDCOVER WITH DUST JACKET

THE FALL OF THE MOGHUL EMPIRE OF HINDUSTAN by H. G. Keene—By the beginning of the nineteenth century, as British and Indian armies under Lake and Wellesley dominated the scene, a little over half a century of conflict brought the Moghul Empire to its knees.

LADY SALE'S AFGHANISTAN by Florentia Sale—An Indomitable Victorian Lady's Account of the Retreat from Kabul During the First Afghan War.

THE CAMPAIGN OF MAGENTA AND SOLFERINO 1859 by Harold Carmichael Wylly—The Decisive Conflict for the Unification of Italy.

FRENCH'S CAVALRY CAMPAIGN by J. G. Maydon—A Special Correspondent's View of British Army Mounted Troops During the Boer War.

CAVALRY AT WATERLOO by Sir Evelyn Wood—British Mounted Troops During the Campaign of 1815.

THE SUBALTERN by George Robert Gleig—The Experiences of an Officer of the 85th Light Infantry During the Peninsular War.

NAPOLEON AT BAY, 1814 by F. Loraine Petre—The Campaigns to the Fall of the First Empire.

NAPOLEON AND THE CAMPAIGN OF 1806 by Colonel Vachée—The Napoleonic Method of Organisation and Command to the Battles of Jena & Auerstädt.

THE COMPLETE ADVENTURES IN THE CONNAUGHT RANGERS by William Grattan—The 88th Regiment during the Napoleonic Wars by a Serving Officer.

BUGLER AND OFFICER OF THE RIFLES by William Green & Harry Smith—With the 95th (Rifles) during the Peninsular & Waterloo Campaigns of the Napoleonic Wars.

NAPOLEONIC WAR STORIES by Sir Arthur Quiller-Couch—Tales of soldiers, spies, battles & sieges from the Peninsular & Waterloo campaigns.

CAPTAIN OF THE 95TH (RIFLES) by Jonathan Leach—An officer of Wellington's sharpshooters during the Peninsular, South of France and Waterloo campaigns of the Napoleonic wars.

RIFLEMAN COSTELLO by Edward Costello—The adventures of a soldier of the 95th (Rifles) in the Peninsular & Waterloo Campaigns of the Napoleonic wars.

LEONAUR

ALSO FROM LEONAUR

AVAILABLE IN SOFTCOVER OR HARDCOVER WITH DUST JACKET

ESCAPE FROM THE FRENCH *by Edward Boys*—A Young Royal Navy Midshipman's Adventures During the Napoleonic War.

THE VOYAGE OF H.M.S. PANDORA *by Edward Edwards R. N. & George Hamilton, edited by Basil Thomson*—In Pursuit of the Mutineers of the Bounty in the South Seas—1790-1791.

MEDUSA *by J. B. Henry Savigny and Alexander Correard and Charlotte-Adélaïde Dard* —Narrative of a Voyage to Senegal in 1816 & The Sufferings of the Picard Family After the Shipwreck of the Medusa.

THE SEA WAR OF 1812 VOLUME 1 *by A. T. Mahan*—A History of the Maritime Conflict.

THE SEA WAR OF 1812 VOLUME 2 *by A. T. Mahan*—A History of the Maritime Conflict.

WETHERELL OF H. M. S. HUSSAR *by John Wetherell*—The Recollections of an Ordinary Seaman of the Royal Navy During the Napoleonic Wars.

THE NAVAL BRIGADE IN NATAL *by C. R. N. Burne*—With the Guns of H. M. S. Terrible & H. M. S. Tartar during the Boer War 1899-1900.

THE VOYAGE OF H. M. S. BOUNTY *by William Bligh*—The True Story of an 18th Century Voyage of Exploration and Mutiny.

SHIPWRECK! *by William Gilly*—The Royal Navy's Disasters at Sea 1793-1849.

KING'S CUTTERS AND SMUGGLERS: 1700-1855 *by E. Keble Chatterton*—A unique period of maritime history-from the beginning of the eighteenth to the middle of the nineteenth century when British seamen risked all to smuggle valuable goods from wool to tea and spirits from and to the Continent.

CONFEDERATE BLOCKADE RUNNER *by John Wilkinson*—The Personal Recollections of an Officer of the Confederate Navy.

NAVAL BATTLES OF THE NAPOLEONIC WARS *by W. H. Fitchett*—Cape St. Vincent, the Nile, Cadiz, Copenhagen, Trafalgar & Others.

PRISONERS OF THE RED DESERT *by R. S. Gwatkin-Williams*—The Adventures of the Crew of the Tara During the First World War.

U-BOAT WAR 1914-1918 *by James B. Connolly/Karl von Schenk*—Two Contrasting Accounts from Both Sides of the Conflict at Sea D uring the Great War.